SHIPS and NARROW GAUGE RAILS

SHIPS and NARROW GAUGE RAILS

The Story of
The Pacific Coast Company

by GERALD M. BEST

Howell-North · Berkeley · California · 1964

SHIPS AND NARROW GAUGE RAILS, the story of the
Pacific Coast Company

Printed and bound in the United States of America.

Library of Congress Catalogue Card No. 64-19122

Jacket and fronticepiece drawing by
Harlan Hiney

Published by Howell-North Books
1050 Parker Street, Berkeley 10, California

Foreword

In the summer of 1920, when I was a cub transmission engineer with Pacific Telephone, I spent my first vacation in the West riding trains and ships. At San Francisco I boarded the steamer *Governor*, flagship of the Admiral Line, and except for a rough afternoon north of the Golden Gate, I enjoyed every minute of the three-day voyage to Victoria, B. C., and through Puget Sound to Seattle. After a round trip by train to Banff and Lake Louise from Seattle, I returned home on the *Governor*. This was the first of many voyages made along the coast through the years, and since I crossed San Francisco Bay almost daily by ferry, I soon became acquainted with the names of other vessels in the coastwise trade.

That same year, in the late fall, I was sent to San Luis Obispo for a week of testing work, and because the equipment failed to show up on time, I had an idle day in a strange town. Being a restless soul, I walked to the Southern Pacific station in the quest of something interesting to watch, and there, parked on a stub-end track to the south of the station was a narrow gauge mixed train with the cars and engine lettered "Pacific Coast." It did not take long to find out that the train was bound for Port San Luis and return, so it was only a matter of buying a ticket and I was aboard the combination coach with half a dozen other passengers. Soon we were backing downhill to the main line, after which we ambled along at a reasonable pace to the sea at Avila, and thence along the shore to a long wharf and the end of the run. The return trip was over all too soon, and every time I drove through San Luis Obispo in later years, I felt impelled to stop and renew my acquaintance with the Pacific Coast Railway. As time went on I watched the gradual deterioration and eventual extinction of what had once been a major factor in the development of the region. It is thus only natural that I should want to set down the story of this not too well known railroad, and since in so doing, I became better acquainted with the

steamship lines and the other railroads belonging to the parent company, the end result has been a history covering all the operations of the Pacific Coast Company.

In this work, I have had the assistance of many wonderful people. Although primarily a railroad hobbyist, I am aware of the fact that a similar group has just as intense an interest in the ships that sail the sea as those of us who love the trains. Without the help of Allan D. Yost of Santa Barbara, who also furnished a monograph on Coastwise Steamship Service by Hugh B. Brittan, as a reference, I could not have reached first base on the steamship roster of the Pacific Coast Steamship Co. Roy D. Graves, Curator of the Marin County Museum and railroad historian as well, has a fine collection of photos of coastwise ships, and I am indebted to him for their use.

The magnificent regional history collection at the San Luis Obispo Public Library was made available to me by Miss Patricia J. Clark, Librarian, and her assistant, Mrs. Mary Hughes Smith. Their complete file of the San Luis Obispo weekly and semi-weekly newspapers dating back to 1868 made it possible for me to get the facts about the Pacific Coast Railway, and the fascinating story of Charles Goodall and his steamship company. In reading these papers I became so interested in the history of the valley that if I seem to include too many local items not directly connected with railroads or ships, it is only because I felt they would add to the value of this story as a regional history. I am deeply grateful to my old friend Herbert C. Grundell, last Manager of the Pacific Coast Ry., for photos and information on the last years of the railroad, to Mr. Wm. T. Smith, President of the San Luis Obispo County Historical Society for his friendly help in locating photographs and data, and to Mrs. Leroy Dart, Curator of the County Museum, for the loan of photographs from the collection. Also to Mr. Vincent Canet of Avila, and long-time resident of San Luis Bay, who has made the history of the Bay and its environs a lifetime hobby.

I am indebted to Capt. Homer G. Benton, formerly of Seattle, for his help in tracing the early history of the railroads later owned by the Pacific Coast Co. in the State of Washington. His paper on the Seattle Coal & Transportation Co. in a recent Bulletin of the Railway and Locomotive Historical Society was a big help, as was a paper by Bruce B. Cheever, a member of the same Society, on Railroad Development in Washington. To my friend Don Roberts of Portland, my thanks for the loan of photos from his collection, and to the others whose names are credited in the photo sections, my thanks and appreciation.

GERALD M. BEST

*Beverly Hills,
California
1964*

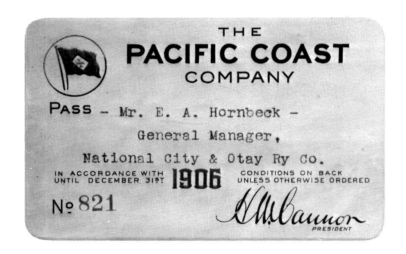

IMPORTANT DATES IN THE HISTORY OF

The Pacific Coast Company

1855	First wharf erected on San Luis Obispo Bay
1867	Goodall, Nelson & Perkins, Agents, organized
9/1869	Peoples Wharf on San Luis Bay opened for business
2/1870	Seattle Coal Co. organized
1/30/1873	San Luis Obispo R.R. organized
7/6/1873	Seattle & Walla Walla R.R. & Transp. Co. organized
9/1873	John Harford's Horse Railroad and Wharf completed
3/2/1874	San Luis Obispo & Santa Maria Valley R.R. organized
2/1875	Goodall, Nelson & Perkins S.S. Co. organized
8/8/1876	San Luis Obispo & Santa Maria Valley R.R. completed
10/17/1876	Pacific Coast Steamship Co. organized
2/1877	Seattle & Walla Walla R.R. & Transp. Co. completed to Renton
2/15/1878	Seattle Coal & Transp. Co. merged with S. & W. W. R.R. & Transp. Co.
2/1880	Oregon Improvement Co. organized
11/26/1880	Columbia & Puget Sound R. R. organized
5/20/1881	Pacific Coast Railroad in California organized
9/1881	Pacific Coast S.S. Co. sold to Oregon Improvement Co. with the San Luis Obispo & Santa Maria Valley R.R.
8/19/1882	Puget Sound Shore R.R. organized
9/25/1882	Pacific Coast Ry. organized by merger of Pacific Coast R.R. and the San Luis Obispo & Santa Maria Valley
10/11/1882	Pacific Coast Ry. extension from San Luis Obispo to Los Alamos completed
3/1883	New line, Port Harford to Avila completed
1885	C. & P. S. branch to Franklin, Wash. completed
9/28/1887	Port Townsend Southern R.R. organized
11/16/1887	Extension of Pac. Coast Ry., Los Alamos to Los Olivos completed
9/11/1890	Olympia & Chehalis Valley R.R. purchased by Port Townsend Southern
8/1/1891	Seattle & Northern R. R. completed
5/4/1894	Southern Pacific R. R. completed, San Francisco to San Luis Obispo
10/1/1895	Oregon Improvement Co. receiver appointed
12/1/1897	Pacific Coast Co. organized. C. & P. S. standard gauging completed
2/28/1899	Seattle & Northern R.R. sold to the Seattle & Montana R.R.
4/1899	Union Sugar Co. factory at Betteravia, Calif. opened
3/21/1900	Oil discovered near Arroyo Grande, Calif.
3/31/1901	Southern Pacific R.R. completed, San Francisco to Los Angeles
9/15/1902	Goodall, Perkins & Co. retire as agents for the Pacific Coast S.S. Co.
11/29/1902	Port Townsend Southern leased to the Northern Pacific R.R.
2/1906	C. & P. S. main line, Argo to Maple Valley leased to Milwaukee R. R.
4/15/1906	Pacific Coast Ry. branch to Suey opened and electrified

6/1909	Pacific Coast Ry. electric line to Guadalupe and Betteravia completed
3/23/1916	Columbia & Puget Sound R.R. name changed to Pacific Coast Railroad
10/1916	Pacific Coast S.S. Co. sold to H. F. Alexander
1918	Lawson branch of Pacific Coast R.R. abandoned
1928	Interurban electric line, Santa Maria to Guadalupe service discontinued
1931	Kummer branch, Pacific Coast R.R. abandoned
1933	Newcastle-Renton branch, Pacific Coast R.R. abandoned
1936	Los Olivos-Los Alamos section, Pacific Coast Ry. tracks removed. 19 miles of Franklin branch, Pacific Coast R.R. abandoned
8/1937	Santa Maria to Guadalupe and Betteravia tracks of Pacific Coast Ry. taken up
3/1940	Palmer Sisquoc branch of Pacific Coast Ry. abandonment authorized
12/20/1941	Pacific Coast Ry. abandoned south of San Luis Obispo
2/28/1942	Pacific Coast Ry., Port San Luis to San Luis Obispo sold
1945	Taylor branch of Pacific Coast R.R. abandoned
1951	Control of Pacific Coast R.R. acquired by Great Northern R.R.

THE MEN WHO OPERATED THE PACIFIC COAST RAILWAY

1875-1876	Dr. John O'Farrell, Supt.
1876-1877	Joseph W. Nesbitt, Supt.
1877-1882	C. A. Haskin, Supt.
1882-1892	J. Millard Fillmore, Manager
1892-1900	C. O. Johnston, Supt.
1900-1910	E. W. Clark, Supt.
1910-1924	J. M. Sims, Supt.
1924-1935	W. T. Masengill, Supt.
1935-1942	H. C. Grundell, Manager

THE PRESIDENTS OF THE PACIFIC COAST RAILWAY

1875-1877	Christopher Nelson, San Francisco
1877-1882	John Rosenfeld, San Francisco
1882-1888	Charles Goodall, San Francisco
1888-1892	George C. Perkins, San Francisco
1892-1895	John L. Howard, San Francisco
1895-1898	C. J. Smith, Seattle
1898-1902	J. D. Farrell, Seattle
1902-1903	Edwin Goodall, San Francisco
1903-1916	J. C. Ford, Seattle
1916-1931	E. C. Ward, Seattle
1931-1941	N. D. Moore, Seattle
1941-1942	G. W. Mertens, Seattle

THE MEN WHO OPERATED THE PACIFIC COAST RAILROAD AND ITS PREDECESSORS

1877-1881	A. A. Denny	President and Manager
1881-1884	J. M. Colman	Superintendent
1884-1885	J. L. Howard	Superintendent
1885-1888	T. J. Milner	Superintendent
1888-1891	H. W. McNeill	Manager
1891-1898	C. J. Smith	Manager
1898-1902	J. D. Farrell	Manager
1902-1916	J. C. Ford	President and Manager
1916-1943	G. W. Mertens	Manager, then Superintendent and Vice-President, later Pres. and Supt.
1943-1948	E. W. Maxwell	Superintendent
1948-1952	H. D. Lear	Superintendent
1952 to date	—	Operated by the Great Northern R.R.

Contents

San Luis Obispo Bay's first landing places. Original wharf, built in 1855 at the foot of this bluff *(above)*, was known as Cave Landing, for the natural cave visible. There was a warehouse on the bluff, to which passengers and freight were lifted by a derrick elevator. After 1864 this landing was known as Mallagh's Wharf, for its new owner.

Remains of 1800 foot Peoples Wharf, completed in 1869, can now be seen only when tide is exceptionally low *(below)*. Present day Avila Pier is in background. — *Vincent Canet*

PART I—DEVELOPMENT OF THE PACIFIC COAST RAILWAY

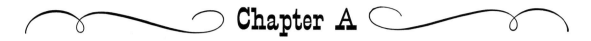

Chapter A

John Harford's Horse Railroad

ALONG THE CENTRAL California coast, halfway between San Francisco and San Diego, extending from twenty to thirty miles inland are a series of valleys and rolling hills, comprising one of the richest farming areas in the State. At its northern and southern extremities the Franciscan Fathers, headed by Junipero Serra erected two missions, San Luis Obispo in 1772 and Santa Ynez in 1804. Both were on the El Camino Real, a horse trail built by the Franciscans for a distance of nearly seven hundred miles along the Pacific Coast.

In 1850, when California was admitted to the Union, San Luis Obispo County had a population of 336 persons, there being only a few large ranchos with their owners, families and employees. The southern valleys near Mission Santa Ynez were in Santa Barbara County, and had even fewer inhabitants, being separated from Santa Barbara town by a high range of mountains which made land travel slow and difficult. One of the earliest settlers north of the Santa Maria River, which divides the region into almost equal parts, was Capt. William G. Dana, cousin of Richard Henry Dana, author of that famous narrative of the sea, "Two Years Before the Mast." Capt. Dana preceded his cousin by eight years, making his first voyage from Boston to the Pacific in 1826, in command of the brig *Waverly*, and after engaging in the Sandwich Islands trade for a number of years, became a naturalized citizen of Mexico in 1835 in order to own land, obtaining a grant of 37,887 acres called the Nipomo Rancho. There in 1839, Capt. Dana built an adobe house and raised a family of 21 children. Today the Dana adobe is in the process of restoration, to become one of the County's treasured shrines. One of Capt. Dana's sons, John

Francis Dana, born in 1837, became a prominent figure in the community and in due time helped sponsor a railroad. Another early settler was E. W. Steele, who bought the Corral De Piedra Rancho, and introduced dairy farming to a region which had been a wilderness. He stocked his ranch with six hundred cows, employed a hundred men and with the Danas and other pioneer settlers began the work of turning the land into a cattle and grain raising paradise.

There were two bays or sheltered beaches along the coast between Point San Luis and Point Arguello, of which San Luis Obispo Bay was the best suited for constructing a wharf where ships could load or unload freight and passengers, while Point Sal Landing, in the lee of that point, could serve the Santa Maria and Santa Ynez valleys. San Luis Obispo Bay offered better protection from the weather than the latter, and here in 1855, Barkley Clements and Charles T. Rommie leased a few acres of beach land, including a rocky promontory, from the Avila family, who owned all the land for miles along the shore of the Bay.

The location was about a mile south of the present town of Avila, and in the lee of a spit of land known as Fossil Point. Here a wharf was erected, and on the steep bluff overlooking the wharf they built a warehouse, with a derrick type elevator to lift both passengers and freight from the wharf to the warehouse platform. The water was too shallow for ships to tie up to the wharf, so it was necessary to transfer passengers or freight to and from the ships in lighters. From this wharf, first known as Cave Landing, passengers bound for the small village which had grown up around Mission San Luis Obispo had to ride in stage coaches over a

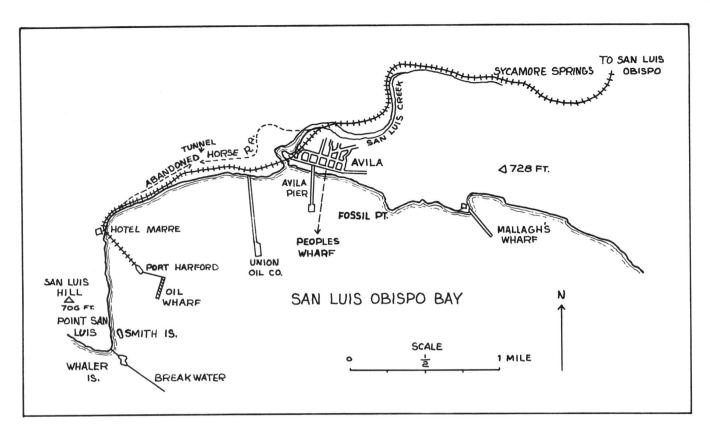

SAN LUIS OBISPO BAY

TO SAN LUIS OBISPO

SYCAMORE SPRINGS

SAN LUIS CREEK

AVILA

△ 728 FT.

TUNNEL

ABANDONED HORSE R.R.

AVILA PIER

FOSSIL PT.

MALLAGH'S WHARF

HOTEL MARRE

PEOPLES WHARF

PORT HARFORD

UNION OIL CO.

SAN LUIS HILL △ 706 FT.

OIL WHARF

POINT SAN LUIS

SMITH IS.

WHALER IS.

BREAK WATER

N

SCALE
0   ½   1 MILE

Present day Avila lies at the mouth of San Luis Creek, with its pier extending into the bay. The Union Oil Company wharf, beyond, is longer. Against Point San Luis can be seen the railroad wharf. Tracks leading from there twice cross the creek. — *Collection of Vincent Canet*

bumpy, sometimes dusty and often muddy road. It was the accustomed way of life of the times, however, and for ten years the wharf continued as the only landing at San Luis Bay. Clements sold his share to John C. Cissna in 1860, then Borland and Bunce bought the wharf and operated it until in September, 1864, they sold it to Capt. David P. Mallagh, who improved the wharf and road leading to the county highway at the mouth of San Luis Creek. This made travel a bit easier for the settlers, who promptly dubbed the landing "Mallagh's Wharf."

Disliking the slow and tedious business of unloading merchandise, especially lumber, at Mallagh's Wharf, a group of merchants led by John Harford of the lumber firm of Schwartz, Harford & Co., the Goldtree brothers and A. Blochman & Co., all of San Luis Obispo, formed the Peoples Wharf Co. in December 1868. Building a new wharf south of San Luis Creek, about a city block south of the present Avila Beach State Park pier, they extended it 1800 feet into the Bay, in water deep enough to permit most steamers to tie up to the wharf and handle cargo with the ships' cargo booms. A narrow gauge railroad was built from the outer end of the wharf to a point far enough inland where a warehouse could be erected, and horse-drawn flatcars handled the traffic to and from the wharf. Completed in September 1869, it failed in its primary purpose, for Capt. Mallagh had a contract with the passenger steamers; naturally most of the freight business and the passenger trade continued to come to his wharf. Not so with the lumber, for Harford controlled the lumber trade, and the schooners bringing lumber always used the Peoples Wharf. The income from lumber was not enough to suit some of the owners, resulting in a quarrel between Blochman and the Goldtrees over the management of the wharf. In November 1872 Blochman sued the Goldtrees, the presiding judge dissolved the Company and ordered it sold at auction in front of the warehouse at the beach. John Harford, having successfully avoided involvement in either the quarrel or the lawsuit, joined with several other San Luis Obispo merchants and Capt. John Ingalls of the Pacific Mail steamer *Orizaba* in a pooled bid at the auction, and were successful in outbidding the others.

At Harford's suggestion, the new owners made a deal with Capt. Mallagh, and appointed him manager of the new Peoples Wharf Co., with the result that Mallagh abandoned operations at Cave Landing, brought his steamer business over to the Peoples Wharf, and Mallagh's Wharf quickly fell into disuse. All ships now used Peoples Wharf, and competition for the time being was at an end.

When the Peoples Wharf was first proposed in 1868, Harford had suggested that it be constructed in the lee of Point San Luis, where the end of the Bay was so well protected by the Point that even in the severest of storms the water was relatively quiet. Frequently ships were unable to anchor near Mallagh's Wharf, and rode out bad weather in back of the Point in perfect security. Harford's partners ridiculed this suggestion, claiming that a road along nearly two miles of rocky shore would cost more than the wharf itself, and insisted on the location near San Luis Creek. They probably also figured that Harford was advocating his plan because he had purchased the entire shoreline from the Point to the creek, from the Avila family in 1867, and stood to make a handsome profit if his plan was adopted.

Late in 1871, a year before the sale of the Peoples Wharf, Harford decided to go ahead with his own idea independent of anyone else, and selecting a site for the wharf, he hired a few men including a surveyor and began the grading for a horse railroad, a distance of two miles from the projected new wharf to the flats of San Luis Creek, a half-mile from the sea. To quote Harford in a letter he wrote to the San Luis Obispo *Tribune* in 1875, "I invested my limited means in the purchase of the land and the making of a grade, and steadily pursued my purpose until the present railroad project became a success." Harford did indeed build his wharf, reaching 540 feet out from the rocky shore where the water averaged fifteen feet in depth. From the end of the wharf to the flats of San Luis Creek he built a 30-inch gauge railroad, using light 15-pound rail, and though the motive power was not steam, it was nevertheless one of the first narrow gauge railroads in the State. In something less than two thousand feet from the land end of the wharf, his railroad climbed eighty feet to the top of the bluffs, then through a tunnel in the rocky cliffs, along the ridge at an even grade

Remains of John Harford's old horse railroad came to light in 1962, almost eighty years after the old tunnel was sealed off. The old track was first used for horse and gravity operation; later steam engines pulled loads over its tortuous grades. In 1883 a lower, leveler track was constructed, along a right of way which ultimately became a road.

until the valley of San Luis Creek was reached, thence down a winding grade to the flats not far from the Peoples Wharf warehouse and terminal. He had little assistance from anyone except his hired crew, preferring to take his time and thereby pay for the work out of income.

By the time the wharf and railroad were completed in September 1873, ten flat cars, one equipped with benches and railings for passenger service, had arrived by steamer from San Francisco, and Harford invited the Editor of the *Tribune* to come down to the harbor and see for himself what had been accomplished. The Editor described in detail a ride over the line from the end of the wagon road, the host being "Honest John" Harford himself. Horses pulled the single passenger car up the hill to the summit, where they were unhitched. The car then coasted through the tunnel, down the steep hill to the water's edge and around the curve at the entrance to the wharf, stopping smartly at the end in true gravity railroad style. Harford had probably never seen such a railroad, but he had worked out the details in remarkably good fashion. The Editor saw freight being loaded on flatcars, with spans of six horses to haul the cars to the summit, where they were cut off and the cars coasted down to San Luis flats. Trains of three cars were customary, the brakemen quickly acquiring skill in braking the cars down the two hills, for there is no mention of any serious accident or derailment during the years of horse motive power on the railroad. A horse fell off one of the trestles shortly after the road began operating, and another time a large bundle of shingles fell down between the rails and stopped the train almost instantly, shaking up the passengers seated on the last car, but these were minor incidents.

All of this activity was not lost on the steamship companies, nor on the businessmen of San Luis Obispo. Harford now wishing to sell his share of the Peoples Wharf, and the other partners being agreeable, found a customer in the firm of Blochman & Cerf, whose feuding with the Goldtree Bros.

had caused its forced sale in 1872. They bought the wharf outright, and realizing what serious competition Harford was going to give them, extended it to deeper water, permitting the largest steamships then in coastwise trade to dock there.

Three steamship lines called at Peoples Wharf at that time, the largest being the Pacific Mail S. S. Co., and the others were the ships of Goodall, Nelson & Perkins of San Francisco, and John Wright, Jr., known as the "Opposition Pirate," who cheerfully undercut the other two lines at every opportunity. Pacific Mail was quick to see the advantage of Harford's Wharf, and signed a contract with him in October 1873, appointing him their agent, and the steamers *Senator, Mohongo,* and *Gipsy* called regularly at Harford's Wharf. "Pirate" Wright also moved over to Harford's with his lone ship, the steamer *William Taber,* but Goodall, Nelson & Perkins rented Peoples Wharf from its new owners for a term of five years, and with their steamers *Ventura, Constantine, Kalorama,* and *Monterey,* they began a rate war which was the natural result of too much competition.

Within two months the passenger fares on any of the ships had been reduced to ridiculously low figures; $5.00 first class from San Francisco to San Diego including meals, and proportionately low fares for intermediate stops. All this stimulated travel; even the lowest paid ranch hand could now afford a trip to the big city by the Golden Gate, and there were reports of passengers packed like sardines in the cabins on some of the ships, with as many as ninety landing at Harford's Wharf at one time. Harford boasted that he had effected a reduction of fifty cents a ton on all outbound freight, and that he had given the community the benefit of competition. His initiative had also stimulated the formation of a company to build a steam railroad from San Luis Obispo to the Bay, something which Harford said was in his mind from the start, but with the completion of his horse railroad he was content to rest awhile and let the steam railroad project worry someone else.

Port Harford, with steamer *Santa Rosa* at the wharf and special train leaving the station at the Hotel Marre.

The line's first engine, AVILA, looked like this when Baldwin built it on a rush order for a double-ender. It needed no tender, for cordwood was stowed in the cab, water in the saddle tank. — *Ward Kimball*

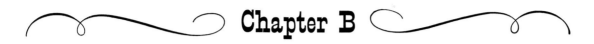

Chapter B

The Steam Railroad to San Luis Obispo

The Paper Railroad

IN THE WINTER of 1872-73, enough attention had been drawn to John Harford's activities to cause a group of ranchers and merchants in the San Luis valley to make plans for a locomotive railroad from the harbor to San Luis Obispo. With the backing of three San Franciscans, William W. Stowe, Henry B. Tichenor and William W. Chapman, these men organized a company to be called the San Luis Obispo R. R. on January 30, 1873, and engaged Hubert C. Ward, a civil engineer of considerable reputation to prepare an estimate of the road's cost. His report was made public on April 19, 1873, and on that same day the first publicity about the new company was released. David C. Norcross was to be the President; Ralph W. Dana, Treasurer; C. H. Phillips, Secretary; and the Directors, besides the three San Franciscans, were Charles W. Dana of the Nipomo Rancho, Edgar W. Steele and William L. Beebe, the latter a partner in Harford's lumber enterprise.

Surveyor Ward estimated that a 30-inch gauge railroad could be built from town to a connection with Harford's horse railroad of the same gauge, including two locomotives, 18 freight cars, 40 timber cars and a passenger coach, all at a total cost of $140,000. He recommended that Harford's wharf be the only one considered, as it was the one all-year steamship landing in the Bay. In his estimate was included the cost of re-laying the horse railroad with heavier rail, and by lowering the floor in the tunnel, steam locomotives could pass through with their trains to the wharf without difficulty.

Harford was in no way connected with the San Luis Obispo R. R., although he did agree to sell

them ties at fifteen cents each, delivered along the right-of-way. Judging by letters he wrote to the newspapers, he appears to have been vastly amused by the grandiose plans of the Norcross group. Rights-of-way were secured by Norcross over the entire route Ward had recommended, and grading was begun a few weeks after the Ward report was accepted. After roughly staking out the line, a show of digging here and there was made; then all work ceased. When Harford's horse railroad went into service in September 1873, he jestingly called it the "San Luis Obispo Railroad", as if Norcross and his group did not even exist. Yet when the Bank of San Luis Obispo opened its doors October 15, 1873, Harford was one of its directors, together with most of the men who had organized the steam railroad, so they were obviously all good friends.

The San Luis Obispo & Santa Maria Valley R. R.

The rivalry between the steamship lines and the two wharves went on all through the winter of 1873-74, and everyone except John Harford was losing money. As the Editor of the *Tribune* said at the time, "whether one steamship company eats up or buys out the other or both continue, in any case our citizens will be well served." For the time being he was right, but he did not realize that the devastating results of too many steamship companies and cut-rate fares was not being lost on Charles Goodall of San Francisco, who had ample financial backing and great plans for expanding his coastwise steamship line. Goodall knew that the great ranchos south of San Luis Obispo were a potential gold mine if their output of grain, cattle, and dairy products could be increased to full capacity by building a railroad through their lands, and since he had plenty of influence in the State Capitol at Sacramento, it was relatively easy to have an enabling act passed by the Legislature. Introduced March 2, 1874 by State Senator Wm. J. Graves, it authorized the formation of the San Luis Obispo & Santa Maria Valley R. R. for the purpose of constructing a railroad from San Luis Bay to the valley of the Santa Maria River, and on through Santa Barbara County to Santa Barbara itself. The bill was passed and signed by the Governor, over the protest of the farm granges involved, for they claimed the granting of the charter would create a transportation monopoly.

The Governor's signature was not yet dry when the Board of Directors of the proposed railroad met in Goodall's office in San Francisco and elected Christopher Nelson, the President. Except for San Franciscans Nelson and Goodall, all the directors were from the San Luis valley, including J. V. Avila, Nathan Goldtree, H. M. Newhall the auctioneer, John M. Price of the Pismo Rancho, F. M. Weinsinger and Dr. John O'Farrell. The latter was voted Superintendent of Construction, and he agreed to run the railroad when it was finished. Fares were fixed at eight cents per mile for passengers and fifteen cents per ton mile for freight, the legislation calling for the road to be commenced within a year, and to be completed a distance of 28 miles within four years. Newspapers promptly commented that 28 miles would get the road to Arroyo Grande, not to the Santa Maria River, but agreed that a railroad even that far would be most welcome.

The ramifications of this bold move on the part of Goodall were many. The Goodall, Nelson & Perkins Line bought a secondhand steamer named the *Los Angeles* and placed it on the San Francisco-San Diego run. It made its first call at the Peoples Wharf on July 4, 1874, making the run nonstop from San Francisco in twenty hours, a record for that time. That same month, the Avila brothers announced the formation of a town near the end of Harford's horse railroad, to be called Avila.

Streets were laid out and lots were sold on very liberal terms. Avila came into being July 18, 1874 and remains today as a monument to one of the earliest families in the region.

As soon as David Norcross and the backers of the San Luis Obispo R. R. realized how their now dormant project was being threatened, they came out of their corner breathing fire, and with as many men as they could assemble, created a tremendous display of activity for several weeks. Beginning work back of the Peoples Wharf warehouse, they dug a grade along the banks of San Luis Creek for over a mile towards San Luis Obispo, but lacking rails, ties, spikes and other materials for track construction, their efforts availed them nothing.

Charles Goodall came down to San Luis Obispo as soon as he heard of the renewed activity of the rival to his proposed railroad. He had just been elected to the Board of Directors of Pacific Mail S. S. Co., which used Harford's wharf. Since Harford was the agent for that company and needed Pacific Mail's business, Goodall held all the trumps. He offered Harford the sum of $30,000 cash for the wharf and his railroad, and as Harford wrote later in his revealing letter to the *Tribune* . . . "I had been fighting Capt. Mallagh of the Peoples Wharf, a rival steamship company and the Avila family, and I had no choice." He accepted Goodall's offer and sold out, remaining in possession of all the land, less a right-of-way across it *for railroad purposes only*. The wisdom of this transaction was to redound to the owner of that land years later, but it was not John Harford. As a bonus, Harford was made a Director of the San Luis Obispo & Santa Maria Valley R. R.

Goodall then began buying a right-of-way parallel to that of the San Luis Obispo R. R., sending down a gang of Chinese laborers from San Francisco to start work immediately. Now these were experienced railroad builders; they had worked for years building the Central Pacific Railroad, and were a far cry from the inept group of ranch hands recruited by Norcross from the countryside. As soon as the Chinese began work, quickly demonstrating that they knew their business, the opposition folded and in a matter of days Norcross and his supporters signed over their right-of-way, merging their paper railroad with the San Luis Obispo & Santa Maria Valley R. R., a name too long for anyone to remember, let alone say. With the competition scuttled, construction of what the local gentry now dubbed the "G.N.&P.", or simply "The Railroad" began in earnest. L. M. Shortt, a well known civil engineer, and R. E. Osgood, an expert with the Howe Truss type of bridge, were brought down from San Francisco. Shortt quickly vetoed the idea of a 30-inch gauge track, and ordered a large amount of 42 lb. (to the yard) iron rail for a 36-inch gauge line. Osgood began work on a trestle nearly four hundred feet long and fifty feet high at one end, designed to bring Harford's railroad from the bluffs down to San Luis Creek on a shorter and less tortuous route. And in San Luis Obispo, things were looking up. The town had a bank, the Western Union Telegraph line was completed to San Francisco, with a branch to Harford's Wharf, and the Cosmopolitan Hotel, the first large hotel in the valley opened its doors on November 14, 1874. Work on the railroad grade progressed all winter, but no rails were laid and no equipment ordered.

In February 1875, Goodall, Nelson & Perkins organized a steamship company of the same name, into which the ships already operated by them as agents were transferred, and the nickname "G.N. & P." line now became a fact. Little had been accomplished on the railroad by May, 1875 other than the preliminary grading for three miles inland towards San Luis Obispo, although Osgood was working on the great trestle, and rights-of-way were being acquired all the way to Central City, as Santa Maria was then called. Owners of all the large ranchos donated a strip of land through their properties; the Steele Brothers giving a four mile section through their Corral De Piedra Rancho, the Dana Brothers a 14 mile long strip through their Nipomo Rancho, while others either gave the right to build through their properties or sold it for a small fee. The Avilas donated land for a station in their new town, and owners of the land at the junction of the Avila-San Luis Obispo wagon road with another road coming up from Pismo and the south, announced the opening of a town there, to be called Harford. Since a rancher named Castro lived at the road junction, the locals persisted in calling the new town "Castro's Place", and eventually the name "Harford" was dropped. In later years it was called "Miles Station", and other than a few houses for the men working at the warehouse there, the town was never built.

The Editor of the *Tribune* delivered salvo after salvo of grumbling editorials in the early summer of 1875, the goat being John Harford, "The Lion" as he was often called, claiming quite truthfully as it turned out, that no equipment had been ordered, no rails had been laid and that the whole project

Miles Station, known as Castro's place when grain was still hauled there from the south. Originally it was named Harford, for a planned community nearby which never developed. — *Vincent Canet*

was a monumental hoax. This produced a rise out of John Harford, who wrote the Editor that he had nothing to do with the railroad even though he had been named a Director; that he had sold his railroad to Charles Goodall and "friends", and that he was quite content to sit back and enjoy the fishing off the Railroad Wharf. Nevertheless, the editorials produced more concrete results than letters, for an order was received at the Baldwin Locomotive Works in Philadelphia on July 16, 1875 for one locomotive, to be named the AVILA and equipped to run in either direction without the necessity of turning around. In other words, it was a double-ender in railroad parlance, with headlights and cowcatchers on both ends, and good visibility for the engineer in either direction. The word "Urgent" was written on the specification sheet and urgent was the word at Baldwin, for the engine was tried out at the factory on August 25th, six weeks later, and shipped by rail to San Francisco the following week. Of 2-4-2 wheel arrangement, with saddle tank on the boiler for water, and ample space in the cab for cordwood, this engine was unique in that it was the first locomotive of this design to be built at Baldwin.

Urgent though the order was, the engine was not unloaded at Harford's Wharf until November 8, 1875, at which time ten boxcars and a passenger coach from the Kimball Mfg. Co., of San Francisco were also landed. Enough rail for several miles of track also arrived, and tracklaying was begun immediately. J. M. Nesbitt, an experienced railroad man was hired to boss the job. Under his guidance the rails reached Castro's Station early in December 1875, and there the work came to a complete halt. Using Dr. O'Farrell as his spokesman, Goodall now applied the well known squeeze. He had watched the owners of most of the vacant real estate in San Luis Obispo, including banker C. H. Phillips, owner of the best unsold lots, the Steeles and the Murphy brothers, just to name a few, reap a harvest in the sale of building lots near the site of the railroad station on Higuera Street. The silver voiced auctioneer, H. M. Newhall, who had been one of the backers of the defunct San Luis Obispo R. R. had sold many a choice site for a store or a residence on the strength of the tremendous growth in real estate values which the railroad would create, once it had arrived in town.

Dr. O'Farrell announced that the cost of the railroad to Castro's had used up all the ready cash, and unless the good citizens of San Luis Valley came forward and subscribed to $50,000 worth of stock, the road would have to end at Castro's for the time being. He emphasized that besides paying Harford $30,000 for his railroad, part of it had been found to be unusable and had to be replaced by a large timber trestle, all very expensive as the piles had to be brought from Oregon by ship. Since outside capital had financed all but $15,000 of the work accomplished to date, this request seemed reasonable enough and a committee headed by banker Phillips received pledges of $35,000 within a week, with $3,500 more coming in later. Dr. O'Farrell agreed that this money would enable them to resume work, and a new contract was given to Martin & Gorrell of San Francisco to complete the job, over the complaints of local contractors that they had not been allowed to bid on it.

In April 1876 the ties, rail, posts for trestlework and lumber for buildings were unloaded at the wharf, now called Port Harford by all except the diehards in San Luis Obispo. To this, Goodall replied, "You can't have San Luis Obispo at both ends of the railroad!" and continued to call the wharf Port Harford until the oil boom of the 1900s forced the changing of the name to Port San Luis. From May through July, the work of grading and tracklaying from Castro's Station to San Luis Obispo progressed without interruption, and the station at the corner of South and Higuera Streets was not yet completed when the rails were laid in front of it on Monday, August 8, 1876. This did not stop the happy spectators from staging an impromptu celebration when the last rail was spiked down, and except for alignment of track, the railroad was a reality. It was usable only as far as Avila station, as much remained to be done on the roadbed of the horse railroad before the new rolling stock could run over it.

The first public timetable was issued August 17, 1876 and announced two trains daily each way from Avila to San Luis Obispo, with connections by extra train whenever a steamer carrying passengers was due. To celebrate the opening of the road there was a special Sunday train to Madame De La Guerra's picnic grounds near Castro's, with many of the excursionists going on to Avila, where

The line's second engine was the wood burner, JOHN HARFORD.

the steamer *Los Angeles* was moored at Peoples Wharf. The round trip fare was set at $1.00 on Sundays and $1.25 on weekdays. The following Wednesday, all the stockholders as well as those who had donated land for the right-of-way were invited to bring their families and friends to a special free excursion. With 300 people seated on benches mounted on flatcars, the dignitaries being crowded into the passenger coach, the AVILA hauled the cheering crowd down to the harbor. Returning to Madame De La Guerra's, a collation was served, some of the guests danced the waltz and the cotillion to the music of Pico's Brass Band, while the others fortified themselves with food and drink, the latter mostly "Sack", to quote the reporter. Returning home in the late afternoon, the railroad was pronounced a grand success, and the excursions were but the forerunner of many more to come.

Before the road opened, it was obvious that the overworked AVILA would not be able to handle all the traffic expected, so a second locomotive to be named the JOHN HARFORD was ordered from Baldwin in May 1876. A conventional 4-4-0, or "American" type, the JOHN HARFORD came out from Philadelphia at the same time an identical engine was shipped to the Santa Cruz R. R., Engineer Shortt having placed the orders simultaneously. Unloaded

at Port Harford in November 1876, it arrived just in time to go in service over the rebuilt horse railroad. An inspection party came from San Luis Obispo on December 11th, the first day on which a train could be run from Port Harford to San Luis, and reported enthusiastically on what they saw. The wharf had now been extended to deeper water, 1500 feet from shore, and with 17 feet depth at low tide. Buildings for housing perishables had been erected, with offices and a shelter for passengers. Water from a large tank placed high on the mountainside was used to supply the steamers and for fire protection. At the shore end, a turntable and water tank for use of the locomotives had been installed, and the Ocean Hotel, built on a projecting shelf of rock at the center of the curved entrance to the wharf was opened. Catering to steamer passengers waiting for delayed trains or ships, and intended also to be a seaside resort, the Ocean Hotel failed to pay its way and was sold in 1882 to two young Italian settlers, Messrs. Gagliardo and Marre. The name was changed to Hotel Marre, and the combination of good Italian cooking and attractive surroundings soon made the hotel a very popular resort and landmark for over sixty years.

A new timetable was issued March 5, 1877, with Port Harford the terminal, Avila being a stop enroute to and from the wharf. Connections were

Hotel Marre, whose "widow's walk" overlooked Port Harford, was a popular honeymoon spot for years. — *Vincent Canet*

made with steamers landing at either Port Harford or Peoples Wharf, with a running time of fifty minutes between terminals. The center of commerce became the railroad station at San Luis Obispo, where hundreds of wagons loaded with grain from the San Luis valley would deposit their loads at the warehouse, while sheep, cattle, hogs and dairy products formed a large percentage of the outbound freight. Manufactured goods, lumber and coal were brought in from the wharves, and the two locomotives were hard pressed to handle the business. Goodall, Nelson & Perkins Steamship Co., whose name was changed to Pacific Coast S. S. Co. in the fall of 1876, had the lion's share of it, and began to wax fat on the profits.

The railroad had cost $210,000 by the time John Harford had been paid, and to pay a portion of it, a bond issue of $110,000 at 6% was sold, requiring an annual interest payment of $6,600. A surplus of $16,000 was left at the end of the road's first year

of operation, and had business remained good in the next few years, the bond issue could easily have been paid off. But here nature intervened with the great storm of January 15, 1878, which struck the California coast without warning. Accompanied by hurricane force winds and excessively high tides, the Peoples Wharf and the landing at Point Sal were destroyed, while the torrential rains washed out sections of the railroad between the wharf and San Luis Creek. Fortunately, John Harford's confidence in the location of his wharf was fully justified, for it came through the storm intact. Supt. C. A. Haskin, in his first month with the railroad after the untimely death of Supt. Nesbitt, was hard put to maintain service. So much damage was done to the ranchos by this storm that 1878 was a very bad year for the crops.

In addition, the locomotives were proving inadequate to handle heavily loaded freight cars over the old horse railroad section, necessitating two

Dramatic changes over a thirty-year period distinguish these two views north on Front Street, Avila. A lone automobile can be seen in the snarl of parked horse-drawn vehicles, in the early 1900s; the railroad bridge looms in the distance. By 1937 automobiles dominate the scene, but the daily train for the wharf provides a reminder of the past. Further changes can be seen on page 24. — *Vincent Canet*

As seen on a busy summer day, 1962, Front Street, Avila. The railroad is long gone. — *Vincent Canet*

and sometimes three round trips of the engine to haul a train of 10 loaded cars with which the engine started from either terminal. The AVILA was good for only two loads on the grades, so all the heavy work fell on the JOHN HARFORD. After two years of constant use, the latter engine became the victim of the road's first wreck in January of 1879, when the stub switch at Avila Junction, at the start of a ninety degree curve at the foot of the steep grade to the summit was set partly open by an unknown person. Engineer Masterman, gathering speed with six cars loaded with sacks of chrome iron ore, saw the open switch too late to stop. After bouncing along over the ties for a few feet, the engine turned on its side in the sand, while the tender, with Fireman Reed scrambling over the piled-up wood, went over the top of the locomotive, demolishing the cab. Reed sailed fifty feet through the air, landing in the soft sand with hardly a scratch. The cars of ore were wrecked, but the miraculous luck which stayed with the railroad throughout its years left Masterman with serious injuries, but none critical.

The JOHN HARFORD and Masterman were out of service for several months, and a squib in the *Tribune* is worth repeating here. "Masterman and his locomotive are both back in their old places on the railroad and looking well, since the bruises and

scratches received in their track jumping exploit have been smoothed and painted over. 'Low-Water Hogan' as usual has done a very creditable job and has proved himself to be a thorobred locomotive painter as well as engineer and mechanic. The artist who worked on Masterman has done equally well."

Returning to the "Tidal Wave" as the storm of January 1878 was often called, the owners of Peoples Wharf had no funds to rebuild it, and were glad to give a ten year lease to Pacific Mail S. S. Co., which had been using it ever since Goodall's steamers had switched to Harford's Wharf. Pacific Mail paid the rent when due, but refused to make any repairs or terminate the lease, and sent its ships to Port Harford. The fine iron hand of Goodall could be seen in this move, for now the railroad had all the business coming in by sea, as there was not even a footpath between Port Harford and Avila. Notwithstanding this monopoly, the railroad showed a loss in 1880, reflecting another bad crop year. Even so, Goodall felt that there was enough potential traffic south of San Luis Obispo to warrant extending the railroad as planned, and at a meeting held in his office in San Francisco on May 21, 1881, a decision was reached to extend the railroad to Central City and the valley of Los Alamos Creek.

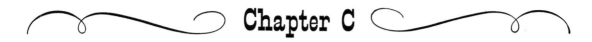

Chapter C

Expansion

THE EXTENSION, being planned by the head of the Pacific Coast S. S. Co., was called the Pacific Coast Railroad to differentiate it from the San Luis Obispo & Santa Maria Valley, and it was built by a separate company, although the officers were the same for both railroads. The announcement of the new company caused a great flurry of activity in San Luis Obispo, and excitement throughout the valleys south of there. Civil engineers came from San Francisco to survey the extension, which was to follow the county road through practically level country for seven miles, then to turn off that road eastward to Reed's Ranch, where it ascended a grade varying from one to three percent through the hills to a summit near Logan. From there it was to descend on a two percent grade through Corbett Canyon to Arroyo Grande.

Once the die had been cast, the building of the railroad to Arroyo Grande was a matter of weeks. Teams commenced the grading in early June, the Chinese tracklayers arrived and began laying track on the north half of South Street in San Luis Obispo to its junction with the county road. Three new locomotives from the Grant Locomotive Works in Paterson, N. J. were unloaded at Port Harford, a newspaper item claiming that these engines had been ordered by the Columbia & Puget Sound R. R. but which were diverted to San Francisco while en route from the factory. Additional platform cars were also unloaded, and the new equipment came just in time to be put to work hauling material to the railhead. By the end of July the track was halfway to Arroyo Grande, which had donated a right-of-way through the town and a site for the station and warehouse.

Beyond Arroyo Grande the roadbed across the Nipomo Rancho was already being graded, while the streets of the town were crowded with wagons hauling grain to the new loading dock. The pile of grain sacks totalled 25,000 by early October, with an equal amount expected before winter. There had been a bumper harvest and without the railroad, the struggle to haul this grain by team to Point Sal would have been hopeless. One can therefore understand the eagerness with which the ranchers walked out along the railroad grade in Corbett Canyon to watch the gang of 350 Chinese working twelve hours a day, laying ties and methodically following up with the rails, then spiking them down. The track reached the station site in Arroyo Grande October 12, 1881, and no sooner had the gang passed the platform than the task of loading the vast accumulation of grain began. Three trainloads a day left for Port Harford, and only the fortunate arrival of 25 new platform cars from Holt Bros. in Stockton, California, made it possible to remove the grain. Supt. Haskin issued a statement that there would be no passenger trains to Arroyo Grande until the wheat had all been removed and the track properly ballasted and aligned. With only one passenger coach, the railroad was in no position to expand passenger service; with freight it was another matter.

New rolling stock had been ordered, and a baggage car, three coaches, a caboose and 35 more platform cars were shipped by steamer from factories in the San Francisco area. Carter of Newark, California furnished the passenger cars, while Holt Bros. built all the new freight equipment. These cars arrived by ship in small lots throughout the

Engine No. 6 *(above)*, gleaming and fresh from the factory, works at the bituminous rock mine near Edna, an important traffic producer for the line. —*San Luis Obispo Public Library*

Engine No. 2 *(below)*, hauling passenger coach to Arroyo Grande, approaches line's only dangerous curve, Horseshoe Bend. — *San Luis Obispo County Museum*

With arrival of three new Grant engines, including No. 4, a larger roundhouse was built in San Luis Obispo, 1882. The new line was finished to Los Alamos in 1883, the year Thompson & West published their *History of San Luis Obispo County,* where appeared this stone print *(below)* of the Henry Hess ranch, Arroyo Grande.

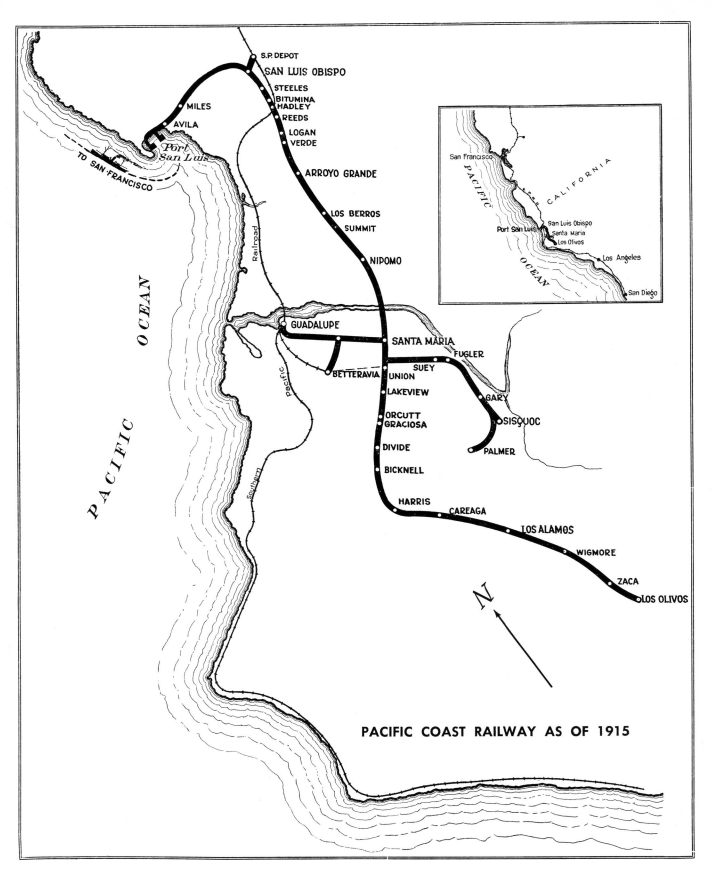

S.P. DEPOT

SAN LUIS OBISPO

STEELES
BITUMINA
HADLEY
REEDS
LOGAN
VERDE

ARROYO GRANDE

LOS BERROS
SUMMIT

NIPOMO

MILES

AVILA

Port
San Luis

TO SAN FRANCISCO

Railroad

Pacific

Southern

PACIFIC OCEAN

GUADALUPE

SANTA MARIA
FUGLER

SUEY
BETTERAVIA UNION

LAKEVIEW

GARY

ORCUTT
GRACIOSA
SISQUOC

DIVIDE
PALMER

BICKNELL

HARRIS
CAREAGA

LOS ALAMOS

WIGMORE

ZACA
LOS OLIVOS

N

PACIFIC COAST RAILWAY AS OF 1915

San Francisco

PACIFIC

CALIFORNIA

San Luis Obispo
Port San Luis
Santa Maria
Los Olivos

Los Angeles

OCEAN

San Diego

spring of 1882, and with five locomotives now on the road, the yards and roundhouse at San Luis Obispo presented a scene of great activity. The original 2-stall roundhouse and 30-foot turntable were now enlarged to six stalls and a 45-foot turntable, one stall being used as a repair track and drop pits for locomotive overhaul.

Regular passenger service to Arroyo Grande was announced on December 10, 1881 and a train left San Luis Obispo daily at 3 P.M., returning from Arroyo Grande at 8 A.M. the next day. Special connections with the steamers at Port Harford were provided, while the stage coach line from the south now terminated at Arroyo Grande. The hard working Chinese graders reached the dry bed of the Santa Maria River on January 14, 1882. Crossing it with a temporary grade consisting of alternate sections of rock fill and drain pipes, a washout was risked rather than delay opening the railroad until a mile-long trestle could be completed. Leaving Arroyo Grande in March 1882, the tracklayers averaged a half-mile a day and arrived at the Santa Maria River in the second week of April. The track gang reached Central City on April 22nd, where a celebration was held as the rails crossed Main Street, the Santa Maria Brass Band providing a festive air for the hundreds of spectators assembled there. Though the Chinese are not notorious beer drinkers, they did not refuse the barrels of the local brew which were offered to them by the jubilant townspeople. According to the Central City *Times* of that date, Roadmaster Masterman, the one-time Casey Jones of the Port Harford line, had come down to witness the event, and took the *Times* reporter back to San Luis Obispo with him in his special train, which consisted of a locomotive and a boxcar fitted out as an office. Masterman related how he and Goodall, while in Central City a few months before, and seeking a site for the railroad station had been told to see Michael Mullee, who owned the plot they wanted. Mullee said, "Sure, take all you want," and signed the agreement on the spot. When asked where they could find something to eat, he pointed to the Delmonico Hotel nearby, and to their astonishment, Mullee, or "Tambo" as he was called by the locals, proved to be the cook and the proprietor as well. Tambo

was tarred and feathered and run out of town on a rail a few months later, but that is another story.

Regular passenger service to Central City, or Santa Maria as it soon became, did not begin until June 1st, on which occasion a special excursion was run from San Luis Obispo to Santa Maria, a large crowd filling all of the new coaches and overflowing onto open flat cars with the inevitable benches. The Nipomo Rancho owners, the Danas, were not to be outdone by Santa Maria, and setting aside a townsite to be called Nipomo, they donated land for a railroad station, warehouse and loading platform. Calling attention to this new town, and no doubt hoping to sell a few building lots in the process, a grand excursion was held on May 6 to Nipomo. A thousand people assembled on the picnic grounds there, easily the largest crowd ever gathered together at one time along the central California coast. The buggies and wagons of the farmers from points as distant as Guadalupe and of course from Santa Maria were lined around the edge of the grove. This was the first of many picnic trains to be run over the new line, the Sunday excursion becoming a part of the lives of almost every resident during the summer months for years to come.

Shortly after Arroyo Grande seethed with excitement over the arrival of the railroad, events directly concerning them were taking place in New York, San Francisco and Seattle, for Henry Villard, President of the Northern Pacific and the Oregon Ry. & Navigation Co. had bought controlling interest in the Pacific Coast Steamship Co., at the same time acquiring most of the stock of the San Luis Obispo & Santa Maria Valley R. R., except for a few shares held by local subscribers. The new extension went with the rest of the package, and Villard announced that it would continue on to Santa Barbara. He told of the development of coal and timber lands in Washington, the ordering of new steamers for the coastwise trade, all under one company to be known as the Oregon Improvement Co., with headquarters in Portland, Oregon. Lumber and coal retailing companies were to be made a part of this group, with offices at the various coastal ports. To head this new company, Villard appointed J. N. Dolph of Portland, while among the directors was none other than George

Arroyo Grande was a thriving community before the turn of the century. The view of the station *(above),* showing wooden bridge, water tank, coaches, boxcar, and horses, dates from 1893. Another view of the bridge *(left)* down the tracks is toward the south. Before 1885 Engine No. 2 *(below)* headed a passenger train there. — *Top and bottom: San Luis Obispo County Museum*

Engine No. 3 and a coach stand at Nipomo station, 1893. — *San Luis Obispo Public Library*

M. Pullman, already famous for his sleeping cars. With control of the railroad and steamship activities having passed from Goodall to Villard, the Editor of the San Luis Obispo *Tribune* refused to be alarmed about it. Assuming a philosophical attitude, he pointed out that the railroad had never been in the hands of the local citizens, and since only $38,500 of the railroad's cost had been subscribed locally, with full half of that amount never paid in, there was no cause for complaint. In fact, to the Editor's thinking, it was an advantage. If there were profits, and losses which would inevitably occur, others in far off places would have the joys or worries accompanying them.

Soon agents of Oregon Improvement Co. were establishing offices for the sale of lumber and coal, while Goodall, Perkins & Co. as their passenger agents were soliciting the transportation of passengers by steamer from Alaska to Mexico and points in between. It was an ambitious plan, and to help carry it out, the new passenger steamer *Queen of the Pacific*, ordered by the Pacific Coast Steamship Co. several years before, but not delivered at that time, was turned out by Wm. Cramp & Sons in Philadelphia. Several other combination freight and passenger ships were purchased, and most of the side-wheelers were either sold or scrapped. The *Ancon* saved them the trouble, for she was lost off the Alaskan coast in early 1883. The *Queen of the Pacific*, loaded with a full passenger list, sailed from Philadelphia early in the summer of 1882, and after circling South America, arrived at Port Harford on August 22, 1882. A special train loaded with sightseers met the steamer at the wharf, open house was held aboard, the champagne flowed and the buffet disappeared like magic as the crowd surged through the new ship and inspected its sumptuous accommodations. A week later, the ship went into regular service on the California Southern route, calling both ways at Port Harford. A new steamer the *City of Puebla*, built for the Ward Havana line in 1881 by the same builders who turned out the *Queen of the Pacific* was purchased in the fall of 1882 by Oregon Improvement Co., and these two sister ships provided the bulk of the service north and south out of Port Harford.

Broken stumps of piles are all that remain to mark the site of the original Avila trestle *(above)*, which served the horse railroad and early steam trains. It was replaced by the truss bridge in 1883. — *Vincent Canet*

The *Queen of the Pacific* lies on her side off the end of the wharf, Port Harford, 1888.

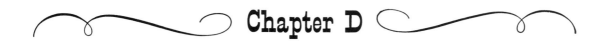

Chapter D

Pacific Coast Railway

THE OREGON IMPROVEMENT CO., soon consolidated all the railroad operations at San Luis Obispo into one company. The Directors of the San Luis Obispo & Santa Maria Valley R. R. and the Pacific Coast R. R., being one and the same, met with representatives of Oregon Improvement Co. in San Francisco and announced the formation of the Pacific Coast Railway Co., to take place September 25, 1882. A bond issue of $1,500,000, to be dated October 1, 1882 would be sold to finance the completion of the railroad to Los Alamos and to pay off previous debts. These bonds were not sold to the public, but were purchased by the Oregon Improvement Co., which already owned most of the stock of the companies involved. The local bankers and merchants were not asked to subscribe to a penny of it, something of a miracle for that day and age, when railroads usually floated additional stock issues and sold bonds at a discount in the communities they served, as a matter of course.

Although Charles Goodall remained as the titular head of the steamship and railroad companies he had founded, a change in management of the railroad was announced at this time. Mr. J. Millard Fillmore, a distant relative of the late President of the United States, for whom he was named, was appointed Manager of the Pacific Coast Ry. Mr. Fillmore bore a fine reputation as an executive and as a gentleman. His father had been a railroad contractor and builder all his working years, his brother J. A. Fillmore was now General Superintendent of the Southern Pacific, and J. Millard Fillmore brought a wealth of experience gained as a construction superintendent for the Delaware, Lackawanna & Western R. R., Trainmaster for the Union Pacific at Laramie, Wyo., Warden of the Wyoming Penitentiary in 1872, Assistant Superintendent of the North Pacific Coast R. R. in 1876, and General Superintendent of the Oregon Ry. & Nav. Co. in 1880. In September 1882 he arrived in San Luis Obispo to take over the management of the railroad from C. A. Haskin, who had been Superintendent for the previous four years.

Fillmore immediately entered into the life of San Luis Obispo in a big way. He purchased land and built a home there, and soon made many friends. Quickly tackling his new job, he travelled over the almost completed line, accompanied by his father who had retired but still took an active interest in railroad building. From Santa Maria the railroad had been built south to the small town of Graciosa, near the mouth of Graciosa Canyon, over practically level terrain, and the 200 foot climb to the end of the canyon and the summit of the grade was accomplished at slightly under 100 feet per mile. From the summit, called Divide, the line descended 100 feet in 5 miles to the Los Alamos creek valley at Harris Ranch. On an easy ascent along the creek, the graders reached the village of Los Alamos on the 1st of October, and the last rail was officially spiked down at what was to be the end of track for six years, on October 11, 1882. A week later the first public timetable signed by J. M. Fillmore, Manager announced passenger service from Port Harford to Los Alamos. Since the new rolling stock ordered earlier was being delivered too slowly to suit Fillmore, wires were dispatched to Carter and other suppliers, and the last coach was unloaded at Port Harford at the end of November. For a few days at least, Mana-

Engine No. 3 (*above*) was the favorite of Manager J. Millard Fillmore. Here it stands in 1888 at Los Alamos station (*below*). This typically unpainted property was the end of the line in 1883.

ger Fillmore used this coach as his private car, for he invited a party of friends to have lunch with him at Santa Maria, and to inspect the new line to Los Alamos. Hauled by No. 3, the new Grant eight-wheeler, this excursion stopped along the line to pick up several of the right-of-way donors, and the party returned to San Luis Obispo praising the smoothness of the ride, and the hospitality of Manager Fillmore.

The large construction gang, having finished building the Santa Maria River trestle, was given a new job which was not easy. The Fillmores had cast one glance at John Harford's old grade over which the road's heaviest locomotives could haul only five loaded cars at one time, and decided that the road would have to be rebuilt from the land end of the wharf at the Hotel Marre, to the end of the trestle at Avila. Wasting no time, and with full permission from San Francisco, he had the new route surveyed and started construction early in January 1883. A partial description of the work is quoted from the San Luis Obispo *Tribune* for January 12, 1883 as follows:

"By the kind invitation of Manager Fillmore, your editor visited the site of the new construction at Port Harford on the 5th inst., accompanied by a party of ladies and gentlemen of this city. The new railroad will follow the beach at an elevation of about 15 ft. above high watermark, allowing one engine to haul 50 loaded cars while now it can haul only 5 over the heavy grade. The place selected for the inauguration of the work was on a high point overlooking the beautiful bay, Point San Luis on the Northwest enclosing it from the ocean, and Point Sal and Point Arguello dimly seen in the south. Back are the high cliffs which form the base of Mt. Buchon. The point was the dwelling place and cemetery of prehistoric Indians whose long-held sacred graves are now to be rudely thrown to the sea to make way for the iron road. Through this old cemetery a deep cut is to be made, and here the work was begun. The honor of throwing the first shovel of earth was accorded to Mrs. Dr. Hayes, the representative of the American Pioneers of our city. The act was most gracefully performed, followed by cheers from the assemblage and the drinking of toasts to the success of the road. After these ceremonies, a party of Chinese laborers were called to the picks and shovels and a search for Indian relics was made. Shells, flints, mortars, pestles, ollas and bones were exhumed. The party then proceeded to Port Harford where the barkentine *William L. Beebe* and two schooners were unloading immense quantites of lumber."

By the end of February the cuts in the rock were finished, and a giant fill, half a mile in length, was built across the marsh at the mouth of San Luis Creek. A new channel for the creek was dredged, and it was crossed by a 300 foot trestle, the only bridge required on the new line. The newspapers recorded the fact that many additional Indian relics had been uncovered, among them a huge mortar nearly two feet in diameter and a foot thick, broken in two, but the pieces fitted and it was easily the largest of its kind ever found in that location. All the relics were assembled in an exhibit at the San Luis Obispo railway station, but today nobody in the city can say what became of them; perhaps they were lost in the 1892 fire at the station.

The new line was officially opened in March 1883, the old grade was abandoned, the rail removed and the portals of the tunnel sealed. In 1963 one end of the tunnel became plainly visible from the shore as the result of roadwork, and pieces of light rail stick out of earth slides which have come down from the old roadbed. John Harford's horse railroad has truly been a long time dying. With the replacement of his old railroad with a new one, Harford seems to have lost interest in San Luis Bay. He sold his land holdings from Avila to Port Harford to the Marre brothers, and among the papers he turned over to them was his copy of the deed for the land used by the railroad, *for railroad purposes only*. This was to plague the railroad and many others in later years, as we shall see. The Marres also rented the Pecho Ranch for a period of years and later bought a large part of it. With their hotel right at the foot of the wharf, and owning all the land in back of the railroad for nearly two miles, they commanded the approach and entrance to the only deepwater pier in the whole region. The wharf was enlarged as a part of the railroad relocation, and a warehouse 40 x 200 ft. was erected

San Luis Obispo station (*above*) in 1894, the year Southern Pacific arrived. The Pacific Coast Railway train for Los Olivos stands at the left. Semaphore and diminutive tower stand where the narrow gauge crossed Southern Pacific at Hadley Crossing (*below*). — *Above: San Luis Obispo Public Library; below: Arthur Alter*

at the outer end, which was widened to 80 feet. Port Harford was now a fully equipped seaport.

With the opening of the entire railroad from Port Harford to Los Alamos, there were two excursions held which were to have an impact on the townspeople of San Luis Obispo and all the villages along the line. A grand excursion from Los Alamos, Santa Maria and Arroyo Grande to San Luis Obispo was held on March 25th and a horde of excursionists descended on a town which was ill-prepared to entertain them. A few brought picnic lunches with them, but the country folks were going to town and expected to dine in a hotel, or at least a restaurant of city proportions. Instead, they found only one restaurant open, and that one a tiny cantina near the station; the hotels were small and the dining rooms were not equipped to entertain large groups. As the railroad management had not informed them of the swarm of visitors who were to descend upon them, they were unable to feed the hungry mob. As a result, the excursionists went home grumbling about the fact that the county seat and chief town was more dead than some of their own sleepy villages, and complained about the lack of a park or place where picnic facilities could be provided.

On the heels of this fiasco, Captain Goodall came down from San Francisco to inspect the completed railroad, and with Manager Fillmore and all of San Luis Obispo's leading citizens aboard the special train, they stopped at each station along the line to inspect the facilities. Arriving at Los Alamos, they repaired to the Union Hotel, where Mr. and Mrs. Fenton, the proprietors, had prepared a superb dinner of roast turkey, rum omelets, excellent wines, café noir and as one member of the party described it, "succotash I have not seen equalled since we feasted with the Onondaga Indians." The tiny village of Los Alamos had shown up San Luis Obispo and the net result of these two excursions was the building of the Hotel Andrews in San Luis Obispo. Headed by J. P. Andrews, President of the Bank of San Luis Obispo, J. Millard Fillmore, Charles Goodall, Louis Marre, General P. W. Murphy, C. H. Phillips, Ernest Cerf and B. Sinsheimer formed the principal group of stockholders in the new hotel. Construction began early in 1884, with accommodations planned for several hundred guests, ample dining facilities for all occa-

sions, and with spacious grounds it was built as a resort, to attract people arriving by steamer to tarry a while, as well as an overnight resting place for transient passengers. Completed July 1, 1885, the Andrews cost $115,000 and at that time was the most expensive building ever erected in the coastal region from Paso Robles to Santa Barbara.

During that famous dinner at Los Alamos other things besides a hotel in San Luis Obispo were being discussed. The Santa Ynez Land & Improvement Co. was proposed with E. W. Steele as President and most of the members of Goodall's party as shareholders. The new company acquired a large tract of land about five miles north of the Santa Ynez Mission, in a district where ranchers had planted groves of olive trees, and which in due time was called Los Olivos. It was planned to stake out a town at a strategic spot in this tract, and to extend the railroad 12 miles from Los Alamos to the new town, where it was expected a large number of easterners who were flocking to California at that time in search of speculative land would buy building lots and settle down in the peace and quiet of the olive groves. The great Land Boom in Southern California was then in full swing, and the fever was so contagious that it was no wonder that Goodall and his friends decided to try their hand at it. All of this was done very quietly and nothing official was announced for over a year after the plans were made. As the crowning jewel there was to be a resort type hotel on a hill overlooking Los Olivos, and plans for this building were drawn by the same architect who designed the Andrews.

PACIFIC COAST RAILWAY CO.
TIME TABLE.

Commencing Apr. 1st, and until further notice, Passenger Trains will run as follows:

SOUTH.				NORTH.	
PASSENGER. A A		STATIONS.		PASSENGER. A A	
LV. PM. 1 30 ar2 10⟩ lv4 00⟩	LV. AM. 8 15 8 50	........Port Harford........	AR. AM. 7 35 7 00	AR. AM. 11 45 11 10⟩ 10 10⟩	
	AR. AM.	........San Luis Obispo........	LV. AM.		
4 55	....	........Arroyo Grande........	....	9 10	
5 35	....	........Nipomo........	....	8 35	
6	....	........Santa Maria........	....	8 05	
6 23	....	........Graciosa........	....	7 45	
6 45	....	........Harris........	....	7 25	
7 1	....	........Los Alamos........	....	7 00	
AR. PM.				LV. AM.	

A—Daily, except Sunday.

Steamship Connections: For steamers Santa Rosa and Queen of the Pacific bound north Los Angeles and Eureka bound south, train leaves depot at 10:30 a. m. for steamers Santa Rosa and Queen of the Pacific bound south and Los Angeles and Eureka bound north, train leaves at 6:20 a. m,

☞ **Notice to Steamer Passengers.**—Passengers for all points between San Francisco and San Diego by all steamers can purchase tickets and secure berths at the office of the Pacific Coast Railway, on Monterey street., up to 5 p. m. of the day previous to steamers sailing from Port Harford and thereafter at the depot till departure of train.   J. M. FILLMORE, Manager.

Hotel Andrews *(above)* was destroyed in San Luis Obispo's worst fire, 1886, despite efforts of volunteer firemen with single hose.

Two years later it was replaced by the Hotel Ramona *(below)*, with convenient horsecar to the railway station. — *San Luis Obispo County Museum*

In the first full year of operation, the Pacific Coast Railway had done as well as could be expected financially. It earned a net of $70,000 in 1884-85 after operating expenses, but of course with $82,200 interest on the bonds, the books showed a deficit. This continued through 1885 and 1886, but as the management worked hard to lower operating expenses, the region began to grow through the migration of thousands of people from other parts of the country. All of this resulted in a surplus of $21,000 after bond interest as of June 30, 1887, and Fillmore's management was really paying off. One of the most profitable operations in the early years of the Los Alamos extension was the Sunday excursion to the picnic grounds there during the spring and summer months.

People in those days had the same urge to go somewhere in the country for an outing that we have today, but they had no automobiles to make it easy. It did not matter to them where they went, as long as they had a train to ride, a picnic at their destination, and a chance to visit with friends. An excursion recorded for posterity in the *Tribune* in May 1883 demonstrated the enthusiasm and eagerness of the populace to ride a train and see the country. At San Luis Obispo, three coaches and a baggage car formed the train, but the crowd was so great that several flatcars, hastily fitted with chairs, then five boxcars with benches were added before all the excursionists were seated. Filled to capacity, the train reached Arroyo Grande, where a flatcar fitted with benches was waiting, with 150 people trying to board it. Somehow they all managed to make it, but at Santa Maria 300 had to be left behind, as there were no more cars, and people were hanging on the steps and even sitting on the roofs of the coaches. To make matters worse, the engine could not haul the 14 cars loaded with 1400 people up the grade in Graciosa Canyon, and had to triple the train up the hill by leaving most of it behind. Setting out the first third at the siding at Divide, two more trips down the hill and back had to be made, rolling the hungry excursionists into Los Alamos over two hours late. Hence there was no time for the Maypole exercises or any other entertainment; everyone had to eat and hasten back to the train. Fortunately, Manager Fillmore had telegraphed to San Luis Obispo and another engine met them at Harris, double-headed the train over the easier south slope of the hill, and arrived back in San Luis Obispo in the fast time of three hours and twenty minutes. This was a typical sample of the many stories of excursions which filled the newspapers at that time, but in spite of the discomforts, they were well patronized and the passenger receipts for the first four years were a sizable portion of the road's gross income.

The railroad was doing very well, but the hotel investment in the Andrews was not, for on a Sunday afternoon, April 18, 1886, the hotel caught fire in the attic, and burned progressively down to the cellar. While so doing, it burned the Bank of San Luis Obispo, the post office, the town's principal livery stable and a number of smaller shops and offices. The fire demonstrated two things: the inadequacy of the volunteer fire department, and the slipshod construction of the hotel. The Editor of the *Tribune* had criticized the hotel's construction in his columns from time to time, calling attention to the amateurish design of the flues leading from the kitchen stoves and the fireplaces. The contractors corrected part of the defects, but several incipient fires in the attic had already occurred, and nothing had been done to eliminate the faults, so in less than a year of service, the Andrews was a heap of ashes, and only heroic work on the part of hundreds of citizens saved the new courthouse from destruction.

April of 1886 marked another "first" in the Pacific Coast Ry.'s history, for they had their first fatality. A tramp named James Perkins, loaded to the eyeballs, mounted the cowcatcher of the excursion train from Los Alamos on that same Sunday of the Andrews fire, and when the train reached Santa Maria, he attempted to get off the engine while the train was still moving. He didn't make it, and efforts of the local doctors failed to save him. The road's perfect safety record had been ruined, and the engine crew came in for severe criticism, though they professed not to have been aware of the freeloader on the head end.

The burning of the Andrews caused the formation of the California Southern Hotel Co., headed by J. Millard Fillmore, and with Goodall, the Steeles, the Marres, Morris Goldtree and R. E. Jack among other backers. Plans called for a fireproof, brick hotel of 300 rooms, on a site where spacious grounds and plenty of room would permit the

Engine No. 101 and the morning passenger train, Los Olivos, 1908.

San Luis Obispo's Commercial Hotel was served by horse-car No. 1 in 1890. — *San Luis Obispo County Museum*

building of the finest hotel in central California. The promoters suggested naming the hotel the Goodall, but the gentleman in question politely declined the honor and said he would prefer the selection of a Spanish name. In due time the hotel was called the Montezuma, until someone called their attention to the fact that Montezuma was an Aztec monarch who hated the Spanish, so the name was changed to Ramona, under which name it was completed and opened with a grand ball and reception on October 3, 1888.

In early 1887 the Santa Ynez Land & Improvement Co., having completed their plans for the town of Los Olivos, persuaded Oregon Improvement Co. to build the 12 mile extension of the railroad from Los Alamos, and after surveys were made, the route was laid out in the summer. A gang of 150 Chinese and 150 locals was hired for the job, and during that fall, the grading and track was completed through the upper reaches of the Los Alamos valley to a summit at 960 ft. above sea level, where the line crossed the divide and dropped down to the edge of the Santa Ynez River Valley at the new townsite, elevation 836 feet. Construction was marked by frequent clashes between the Chinese and the hot-headed whites, ending in a pitched battle two miles west of Los Olivos in which a local ranch hand received a broken head and had to be hospitalized. When the last spike was driven, in front of the site of the Los Olivos station on November 16, 1887, the Chinese were retained to lay out the streets of the new town and do other grading work on the site of the resort hotel which was then under construction. This hotel, called the Los Olivos, was built on a hill overlooking the town, and was completed May 1, 1888, with a grand excursion from San Luis Obispo and Santa Maria to celebrate the occasion. The hotel was filled with visitors, and the newspapers sang with praise for the efforts of Fillmore's group to provide luxury accommodations for passengers using Los Olivos as the transfer point for the Santa Barbara stages. Nothing was said in any newsprint at that time of the Central Hotel, built in 1886 across the street from the site of the Los Olivos station, by Felix Mattei. A private venture, this was a smaller hotel, built by a master hotelman, and except for many additions, stands there to this day as a land-

mark, the only one of its kind, of the days when Los Olivos was a busy transfer point.

We are ahead of the story of Los Olivos and the land exploiters there. No sooner was the railroad completed than a grand auction, free excursion and barbecue were announced by the Santa Ynez Land and Impr. Co. to take place on November 30th. The reporter for the San Luis Obispo *Tribune* describes the auction and what came of it, and is quoted in part here:

"The beautiful rain was on hand in great force last Wednesday morning, to the disgust of the managers of the Los Olivos land sale, who had watched the weather signs for days previously. The steamers arrived from north and south at Port Harford, loaded with passengers destined for the place of sale and they paced the wet decks, balancing themselves against the bounding billows, looking at the discouraging shore, felt the mist and rain, and many of them concluded they did not want land badly enough to 'land', and so remained aboard and went on to San Francisco or Santa Barbara. But a numerous company braved the elements, and promptly at 8 a.m. a double-header pulled out of the San Luis depot with 300 passengers aboard, wet, cold, crowded and uncomfortable. The discomfort could not be helped. The resources of the railroad were all deployed. If the weather had been fine, there were plenty of open cars available, but against the flood, nothing could be done but sit, or stand and suffer and growl. At Los Olivos, everything had been done that was humanly possible for the comfort of the guests. A covered platform had been erected whereon the crowd might stand, for the soil at Los Olivos is deep and rich and the plentiful moisture had readily penetrated it, so the incautious pedestrian could pick up a 25-foot lot on each foot in the course of a short walk. The San Luis Band played, the barbecue smoked and sizzled, there was a plentiful supply of sack, particularly sack, and the crowd recovered its good nature and grew anxious to make a fortune.

Mr. H. O. Weller, the celebrated auctioneer from San Francisco engineered matters, while Mr. C. H. Phillips palavered the congregation and helped them see the millions in the future city that was to grow about them and presently, the lots were put up for sale. Those immediately about the depot being the first offered, a number of choice lots 50 x 140 sold at $390. Then the property around the Los Olivos hotel was offered, and a number of nice lots there were knocked off. But the projectors of the sale were not able to see much in it for them at the prevailing low prices, and concluded to withdraw the rest and wait for brighter days. All told, 29 lots were sold for $6,300, a tiny fraction of what the ambitious promoters had hoped to sell."

Wet, bedraggled and disgusted, the multitude bestowed themselves as best they could on the train, and departed, but a new host of speculators returned again on March 9, 1888, attracted by the exciting ads in the San Francisco and Los Angeles newspapers, and dutifully the Santa Ynez valley poured forth torrents of rain, in such abundance this time that the crowd never left the shelter of the tent, and quite a few remained in the cars throughout the stay there. The land that was sold was almost all farm land in the outlying countryside, about $35,000 being taken in at the auction, but the town of Los Olivos attracted few buyers, and so it was to be from that day henceforth. The Hotel Los Olivos was completed, and was the center of many excursions in the following year, but the town was another matter, and nothing the land company could do or say produced any concrete results. The effort came at almost the end of the great California land boom, and having had their fingers burned in the southern half of the State, the eastern investors in speculative land were a cagey breed, and the rain on the occasion of both auctions killed off the whole project.

In the interim, San Luis Obispo had not been idle. Besides the rapid construction of the new Hotel Ramona, the city was to have a street railway. With Edwin Goodall as President, and J. Millard Fillmore doubling in brass as the Manager, a 3-ft. gauge horse car line was built for a distance of 2½ miles from the Pacific Coast Ry. station, along Higuera Street and Court Street, to Monterey, and up Monterey to Upham Street. By agreement with the merchants along Osos Street, who paid for part of the cost, the line was then continued along Osos and Broad Streets. Five cars, three of the open type and two closed type were built by Holt Bros. in Stockton, with nine horses on the roster as motive power. The railroad was well patronized as a novelty at first, but in 1891 Goodall sold the line to a local group headed by John L. Howard and R. E. Jack, and in 1900, Jack bought the road outright, ran it for a few years, and then sold the rail and equipment for scrap. The streetcar line had proved to be sheer luxury, and most of the townspeople preferred to walk or go by private conveyances.

Various events of the period between the completion of the railroad to Los Olivos in 1888 and the arrival of the Southern Pacific R. R. in 1894 served to enliven things, however. The threat from the north grew month by month as the Southern Pacific colossus extended its coast line railroad nearer and nearer to San Luis Obispo. Reaching Salinas from San Francisco in 1873, the line had been slowly extended as money and equipment was available, until in 1888 the track had reached Templeton, only 24 miles north of the town. The newspapers were filled with ads for the Pacific Coast Stage Co., which extolled the virtues of the stage-rail route, only 13 hours to San Francisco, and stressing the discomforts and the delays of steamship travel.

The Southern Pacific stopped work when it reached Templeton, for the great job of descending from the plateau there, down the slopes of the Cuesta to San Luis Obispo was almost as tough a job as the one they had in 1873-75 when they crossed the Tehachapis from Bakersfield to Los Angeles. The San Luis papers were filled with items about "THE RAILROAD", and they did not mean the narrow gauge Pacific Coast Railway. What had been the only railroad in their lives for fifteen years was now relegated to second place, and there was constant speculation on when the Southern Pacific would reach San Luis, and what its coming would mean to the town. Southern Pacific engineers surveyed the route, and no doubt a plan had been worked out in San Francisco as to when the job would be done, but in the meantime, the local populace had the choice of riding the narrow gauge to Port Harford and braving the high seas to San Francisco, or riding the rock-and-rolling stagecoaches up the steep Cuesta to Templeton, with a long ride on the train to follow.

Advertisements for stage line connecting, over the mountains, with Southern Pacific trains for San Francisco, advised people of San Luis Obispo in 1888 of the supposed disadvantages of travel by sea. — *San Luis Obispo Public Library*

The steamer *Queen of the Pacific* focused all of this dramatically on the morning of May 1, 1888, when at 2 a.m., while 15 miles off Port Harford northbound, water began entering the engine room, and Capt. Alexander made a quick decision to try to make shore and beach the ship rather than abandon it at sea. While the crew manned the pumps and the engineroom fought against the mounting flood, coming from they knew not where, the ship steamed at top speed for Port Harford. When the engines and boilers finally went dead, the Captain had made it to a point about 500 ft. off the end of the wharf, and there the stately ship sank in 22 feet of water, turning over to a sixty degree list, but leaving one side entirely exposed. All 125 passengers, and all of the crew made it to the wharf in lifeboats, and when divers went down two days later to learn the cause of the sinking, they found an open deadlight in a cargo hold at the waterline. Closing it and pumping out the

water, the ship rose to an even keel, and was towed to San Francisco, where it was completely renovated and renamed the *Queen*, under which name it sailed for many years in coastwise service.

Quite naturally, the Pacific Coast Stage Co. owners chuckled mightily at this disaster to their rival, but on July 22, 1888, the stage from Templeton, loaded with passengers from San Francisco rolled into town with the startling news that it had been held up on the Cuesta grade by a highwayman after the most approved Black Bart style. The passengers were robbed of all their valuables, the Wells Fargo strongbox which normally held only bank checks was looted of $2,000 in gold coin, and all by a solitary individual armed with a revolver and possessed with unlimited nerve. There was not a gun on the stage and Jim Myers, the driver, was a picture of disgust as he described how the bandit called "Stop! Stop!", as the stage came across the

By 1891, after two holdups and a bad accident, the comparisons disappeared. — *San Luis Obispo Public Library*

One of the line's best customers was hotelkeeper Felix Mattei, here shown leaving the train. Los Olivos station, which in 1887 became the end of the line, had passenger platform and ornate building.

bridge at Borondo's, in the bright moonlight. The bandit covered the eyes of each passenger with strips of cloth so they could not study him, and while he was a gentleman, he was certainly thorough, and everyone but a douty Missourian named John H. Hayden were stripped clean. Hayden was the last in line, and had time to remove all but one greenback from his wallet and hide it in the heel of his shoe. He was the only one with money when the stage reached town.

A sheriff's posse was sent at once to the scene of the crime, and for days they searched the whole area for clues, with no results. Each stage went out with two shotgun bearers for weeks thereafter, but the bandit kept out of sight, and while suspects were arrested by the dozen, they all had airtight alibis. After a few months, the shotguns were withdrawn because of the expense, and on the very next moonlight night, the robber struck again at the same place, on November 23, 1888, proving that he was a local man. He used the same tactics of blindfolding his victims, but this time they were a poor lot, and he got only $25 in cash and a few watches for his pains. The strongbox had no gold, and the mail pouches had no money in the letters he opened and strewed around, so with obvious disgust the bandit let the stage go on its way.

At the other end of the Pacific Coast Ry., the stagecoach to Santa Barbara had been held up in early November near Los Olivos, and a large haul had been made by a lone bandit, definitely not the Cuesta robber. The stage was held up again in 1890, and the bandit caught by a Los Olivos citizen named Conway, who tracked the gunman through the back country and brought him in two days later. Conway, an insurance agent, collected $1,000 in rewards from Wells Fargo, and as a one-man posse he was the local hero for years to come. He also ended stagecoach robberies along the central California coast for all time. However, none of these events stopped the challenging ads for the stages, until on October 13, 1891, the stage from Templeton came lurching down the Cuesta grade at high speed, overloaded and topheavy, and carelessly driven. On a sharp curve the coach turned over, hurling the driver and four passengers who were riding with him topside, over a cliff to their doom, while everyone inside the coach was seriously injured. New ads for the coaches now stressed

the reduced rates and the faster time to San Francisco, until the arrival of Southern Pacific rails in 1894 erased the stages from the scene.

The two-year-old Hotel Los Olivos, destroyed by fire in 1890, was never rebuilt.

At the time of the sinking of the *Queen of the Pacific*, Charles Goodall stepped down as President of the Pacific Coast Ry. because of ill health, and ex-Senator George C. Perkins, his long-time partner in his enterprises skippered them until the Oregon Improvement Co. failed in 1895. On January 31, 1890, the Hotel Los Olivos was destroyed by fire in the early morning hours, nothing being saved except the grand piano. The last vestige of the land boom thus became ashes, and Los Olivos settled down to relative obscurity. Felix Mattei and his Central Hotel across the street from the railroad station now had full sway, and changing the name to Los Olivos Hotel, he enlarged the building to care for the excursion crowds of the summer season. Reports of 300 passengers were common for the Sunday excursions of that summer; arriving at Los Olivos they would rush to Mattei's dining room, while compliments regarding his cuisine and wine cellar were heard on all sides.

From 1888 through 1893, the narrow gauge averaged $100,000 a year of income before bond interest, with at least a $20,000 surplus turned over to Oregon Improvement Co. A few miles south of San Luis Obispo, near the present town of Edna was a quarry which through the years gave the railroad a large amount of business. An outcropping of bituminous rock, or oil shale as it is called

The big oak tree still stands beside the station at Los Olivos, across the road from Mattei's Tavern.

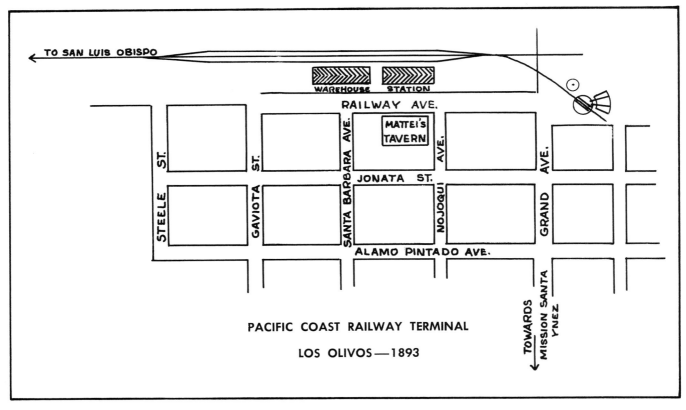

today, was quarried and shipped in sacks by the thousands of tons, forming the base for early paved roads in many parts of the State. When heated and rolled, it formed a sealed and long-lasting pavement. Its presence on the surface was an indication to geologists in later years that large quantities of oil should be under the ground.

In January 1892, Manager J. Millard Fillmore was forced to resign because of ill health, and he died in May of that year at the age of 48. His successor, with the title of Superintendent, instead of Manager was C. O. Johnston, who immediately began a program of renovation of the rolling stock and buildings. The Southern Pacific had resumed construction south of Templeton in 1890, reached Santa Margarita in 1891 and began work on the series of tunnels and cuts through the rock which was to bring the railroad down the Cuesta to San Luis Obispo, a descent of 1100 ft. in 12 miles, from the south end of the summit tunnel. Superintendent Johnston and his superiors knew very well what was going to happen to the passenger business on the steamers northbound out of Port Harford, when the Southern Pacific reached town, and they were bound to lose some of their freight business at the same time.

Disaster struck the Pacific Coast Ry. on November 11, 1892, when an incendiarist set fire to the coach shed and car repair shop in the early morning hours. The lone night watchman sounded the alarm, started the steam operated water pump and manned a fire hose in an effort to snuff out the fire before it became dangerous, to no avail. The volunteer fire department was late in arriving on the scene, and when they finally got there, the car shop was a mass of flames. The great warehouse, full of sacks of grain awaiting shipment to the harbor was already on fire. The only source of water was the storage tank for the locomotives, as no hydrants had been installed within many blocks of the railroad terminal, and so its use was confined to saving the roundhouse, the front half of the station building and the other structures out of the range of the main fire. Such cars as could be pushed away from the flames were moved by sheer manpower, and one by one the locomotives were towed out of the roundhouse by the only engine with steam up. When the fire was out, the losses

were toted and they amounted to four of the road's seven coaches completely destroyed, plus a combination coach, the road's two cabooses, 14 flatcars and a boxcar, most of the flats being loaded with lumber. Besides a large quantity of stored lumber, 1800 sacks of grain went up in smoke, and all that was left was the freight and baggage section of the station, the roundhouse, paint shop and a few small outbuildings. With only a baggage car and three coaches left, Superintendent Johnston fitted out several boxcars with seats hastily sent down from San Francisco, and an order was placed immediately with the J. Hammond Car Works in San Francisco for new rolling stock. By April of 1893 a new coach shed with three stalls, 225 ft. long had been erected, a new warehouse had been built, and the station rebuilt. A new locomotive was ordered from Baldwin, a mogul type similar to the two Grant freight engines, but somewhat heavier. A combination coach, four passenger coaches and a baggage-mail car arrived from San Francisco, and as the old combination had only been partly burned, it was rebuilt, so the railroad now had more passenger rolling stock than ever.

The Southern Pacific reached the site of its station in San Luis Obispo on May 4, 1894, and in a matter of days started through passenger service to San Francisco. The narrow gauge was now no longer a monopoly, and the passengers boarding ships northbound out of Port Harford dropped by a large percentage, particularly in the first weeks before the novelty of riding a train up the Cuesta wore off. The lumber business remained normal, however, as it was still cheaper to ship lumber by steamer from Washington than to haul it by rail. The Southern Pacific made a friendly gesture to the Pacific Coast Ry. and donated land for a warehouse and transfer platform at the Southern Pacific terminal, and a right-of-way for a track to the new passenger station. A spur track from the Pacific Coast Ry. main line on South Street connected the two railroads, and their first timetable showing connection with the Southern Pacific was published November 2, 1894. Efforts were made by both companies to schedule their trains so passengers could come through from the south and make connections without a long wait. There was no turnaround at the Southern Pacific station, so the northbound Pacific Coast Ry. trains headed in to the Southern Pacific, and backed in when they were going south.

The Southern Pacific continued construction of their Coast line south of San Luis Obispo, and by 1896 had reached Casmalia, where construction stopped for a year or more, as the gangs were transferred to work in Southern California. The Southern Pacific had to cross the narrow gauge at Hadley, to which point they had roughly paralleled it. Having been there first, the narrow gauge had the right to dictate the terms of the crossing. A grade crossing was agreed to on condition the Southern Pacific install a tower with suitable signals and derails, and have a man on duty 24 hours a day. The narrow gauge trains were to have the right-of-way, and though the Southern Pacific management smarted under this added expense and restriction, they had no choice. The obvious solution would have been for the Southern Pacific to cross over the narrow gauge with a bridge structure, and ten years later they devoted a lot of

time and effort in a survey of such a crossing, only to conclude it was cheaper to pay the towermen and maintain the status quo. Derails were not installed at first, and in December 1894, the northbound passenger train from Los Olivos had a hairbreadth escape at the crossing, when a loaded gravel car at the end of a Southern Pacific construction train south of the crossing became detached and ran away northbound uncontrolled, missing the last coach of the passenger train by ten feet. Derails were soon installed after this incident, and the narrow gauge train crews could bring their trains across the Southern Pacific without looking fearfully in both directions.

The financial panic of 1893 and the depression which followed it soon had its effect on the narrow gauge, and the towns it served. The Ramona Hotel, which had lost a considerable amount of patronage as soon as the Southern Pacific reached town, closed its doors the day after Christmas, 1894. The hotel had been the social center of the community, and it was sorely missed. The company was reor-

In 1963 Mattei's Tavern was still doing business at the same old stand after seventy-seven years.

ganized, a new Manager was hired and the hotel reopened with a grand ball on July 15, 1895, again taking its place as the leading hotel of the region.

The Pacific Coast Ry. ran up its first deficits of any importance at this time, and in 1895, the Oregon Improvement Co., whose other properties had also suffered heavy losses in the previous two years, defaulted its principal bond issue. A Receiver was appointed, and after the bondholders had approved, the property was sold under foreclosure on November 6, 1897, to the Pacific Coast Co., the new name under which the reorganized properties of Oregon Improvement was to be known. Included in these holdings was the Pacific Coast Ry., the Columbia & Puget Sound R. R., the Seattle & Northern Ry., the Port Townsend Southern R. R. and the Pacific Coast S. S. Co. The coal and timberlands went with the above companies, and on this basis the Pacific Coast Ry. could be said to have gone through the wringer. Operations were directed from Seattle and the officers of the new company served all the units. Accounting for the Pacific Coast Ry. was handled from the Seattle office instead of San Francisco as formerly.

Fires continued to plague Superintendent Johnston, for the tiny, two-stall roundhouse at Los Olivos burned one Sunday afternoon in July 1896, and Engine No. 6, stored dead over the weekend in one of the stalls was almost completely ruined. It was in such bad shape that it had to be brought to San Luis on flat cars, and while it was carried on the roster for another four years, it never again saw service. On another day of that same year, the rear coach on the Port Harford train, unoccupied at the time, caught fire from a red hot stove while en route to the harbor and was partially destroyed. Late in 1897, the Union Sugar Co. acquired a lease on a considerable amount of land in the Santa Maria valley near Guadalupe, and made plans to erect a sugar factory there, with agreements signed with many ranchers to raise sugar beets on their properties. The factory was built on a site called Betteravia, and in February 1898, the Pacific Coast Ry. built a branch line from a point two miles south of the Santa Maria station, a distance of four miles west to the factory site. The Southern Pacific built a three mile branch from Guadalupe,

providing the new factory with two rail connections. A large gang of Chinese laborers built the narrow gauge branch, and were put to work building the factory, which was completed early in 1899. When the factory opened and started processing its first crop of beets, the 225 employees, most of whom lived in Santa Maria, and including 100 Chinese were hauled daily to and from the factory. The Chinese later moved to barracks on the factory grounds. Boxcars fitted with benches formed the nearest thing to a commute train the Pacific Coast Ry. ever had, and of course it was not long before this train was called the "Dead Beet Special".

From 1894, when the Southern Pacific reached San Luis Obispo, until the last spike was driven near Gaviota in 1901, the space between the two railheads was known as "THE GAP". Seemingly ungrateful to the narrow gauge for opening the valley to commerce, the newspapers were filled with speculation on when "THE GAP" would be closed, as if in so doing, the Southern Pacific would release everyone from a prison of which the Pacific Coast Ry. was the jailor. As if to oblige, the Southern Pacific built a branch east from the coast as soon as the rails reached the mouth of the Santa Ynez River at Surf, to the village of Lompoc, nine miles inland, running a through passenger train to San Francisco daily from Lompoc, which was then made the northern terminal for the stage line from Santa Barbara. This bypassed the narrow gauge, and permitted San Franciscans to reach Santa Barbara with only one change, at Lompoc. The daily passenger train on the narrow gauge was promptly cut to a mixed train, and Mattei's Tavern was no longer the busy, overnight stopping place for through travelers. The Tavern did not lose its popularity as a good place to dine and tarry awhile — 65 years later it is still at the same old stand, catering to motorists in search of a quiet spot away from the freeways and the diesel trucks. Its parlors are filled with pictures of stage coach days, with a map on the wall showing the townsite plans of J. Millard Fillmore and his associates in that bygone day when it rained and rained and rained. The Mattei family recently sold the Tavern to Carl Birkholm of nearby Solvang, and the tradition of almost eighty years will be carried on by the new owner.

Chapter E

The Oil Wells Came to Santa Maria

THE LAST YEAR of the 19th Century was the best the farmers had ever seen, for the wheat crop was almost overwhelming. Both railroads worked day and night to haul away the 450,000 sacks of grain, most of which went to Port Harford and thence north or south as fast as the ships could load it. Busy with the harvest, few of the ranchers noticed the small groups of men plodding along the roads, armed with maps and studying the hills and valleys with keen eyes of experienced geologists. For these were oil prospectors, mostly employed by the large oil companies in the southern part of the State, with a few eager wildcatters thrown in. They combed the countryside from Los Alamos on the south, through Santa Maria and Arroyo Grande to San Luis Obispo, and from the remote Huasna valley on the east, to the sea. The Union Oil Co. set up its first derrick at Arroyo Grande, the San Luis Oil Co. drilled further north near the crossing of the railroads at Hadley Tower, the Los Angeles Oil Development Co. leased the Tar Springs Ranch, the Puente Oil Co. leased practically the whole Huasna valley in the hills east of Arroyo Grande and the LaHabra Oil Co. leased the Hasbrouck Ranch near Arroyo Grande. Drilling commenced in earnest, and the first oil was struck on March 21, 1900 in the Huasna valley, miles away from the railroads. It produced only twenty barrels a day, too small to pay, while other wells were drilled deeper but turned out to be dry holes.

(page opposite) By 1913 the railroad wharf at Port San Luis, once Port Harford, had been extended to serve oil tankers. Alongside the railroad warehouse lies the passenger steamer, _Santa Clara._ — Vincent Canet

Oil was found near Arroyo Grande at 500 feet, but also in quantities too small to exploit, and deeper wells were planned.

The last spike of the Southern Pacific Coast line was driven January 9, 1901 near Gaviota, and a train carrying Southern Pacific officials crossed the spot a few hours later. "THE GAP" was now gone, gloated the newspapers, and E. W. Clark, the new Superintendent of the Pacific Coast Ry. who had replaced Johnston in 1900, knew that the passenger business out of Port Harford would soon be finished. Through trains over the Coast line began service March 31, 1901, but after three serious derailments between Santa Barbara and Gaviota in the first months of operation, the Southern Pacific decided to close down the line for through traffic and re-lay the entire track from Santa Barbara to Gaviota, which had been originally laid with light rail and was not standing up under the heavy trains which began to roll over it. "THE GAP" was thus resurrected, and it was not until December 7, 1901 that the _Sunset Limited_ came through San Luis Obispo northbound, the first train since March to go through from Los Angeles to San Francisco over the Coast line.

During 1901, the Western Union Oil Co. leased most of the Careaga Ranch in the Los Alamos valley east of Harris, on the Pacific Coast Ry., and brought in a well in April which produced over 200 barrels of good quality oil a day, without pumping. By January 1902 their second well came in at 2200 ft. and created an emergency for the narrow gauge, for they owned no tank cars and delivery of new cars would take months. Superintendent Clark knew the answer for this one, and

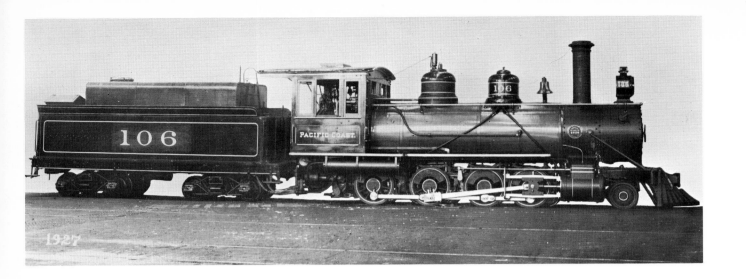

Engine No. 106 was one of five consolidation type engines bought to haul oil from Santa Maria to tidewater. — *Herbert Broadbelt Collection*

Engine No. 107 still had its capped stack when this picture was made at Los Olivos. Fireman Bruno and Engineer Fred Lang lend support.

requested an emergency supply of tanks off standard gauge cars, from the oil companies in Southern California. When they arrived by steamer at Port Harford, flat cars provided by Clark were waiting, to be combined with the tanks to make a practical, though homemade tank car. Ten of these cars were in service within a month, all busy hauling oil from the wooden storage tanks at Careaga siding. To make further use of the Careaga oil, Superintendent Clark converted all the locomotives to burn crude oil instead of coal, beating the Southern Pacific in converting their Coast line locomotives to oil by more than a year. Careaga was made the regular fuel stop for all locomotives, and an oil fueling station was built in San Luis Obispo at Southern Pacific Junction. In October 1902 the Careaga operation had 14 producing wells, some as high as 300 barrels a day and when the oil began accumulating in the storage tanks Superintendent Clark requested more tanks from Los Angeles.

The drillers at Harris, near Careaga, found no oil, but the Pinal Oil Co., a small Santa Maria company which had found oil indications in the hills east of Graciosa Canyon near Graciosa Station, brought in a 400 barrel well, creating a new problem for Superintendent Clark. On June 2, 1903, Pinal Well #3 (the 2nd well had been a dud) came in at 2500 barrels with a force so great that it spewed oil over the top of the derrick. Lacking storage tanks for this monster, Pinal tried to shut down the well, but the casing cracked and when Superintendent Clark hastened back from San Francisco, where he had been meeting with oil officials on the shipping problem, he found oil bubbling out of the ground around Pinal #3 at such a rate that it was flowing down the canyon toward his railroad. Hastily constructing an earth dam across the canyon, an oil lake was formed, temporarily relieving the crisis, but the busy Pinal drillers, like the school boy who sticks his finger in the drinking fountain, had been drilling a fourth well and deepening their first; both came in on the same day as gushers, creating the utmost confusion. In sympathy, Pinal #3 went on a rampage again, blew off its cap and sent the derrick across the canyon, wrecking the bunkhouse and flooding the whole area with oil.

Standard Oil Co., which had just contracted to buy all the oil that Pinal and the other small independents could produce, had shipped large storage tanks from their Bakersfield properties and were hastily erecting them at Port Harford to store the oil as it was brought in by the railroad. Tanks for the narrow gauge flatcars arrived on every ship and an order was telegraphed to the Baldwin Locomotive Works for three consolidation type locomotives, the first of which, No. 105, arrived on May 13, 1904. The road at that time had only five locomotives, three of which were considered freight engines. Two lighter engines, both 4-4-0s, were hauling the passenger and mixed trains, and when any engine was withdrawn for repairs, the load fell on the remaining four. Breakdowns on the road, a rare occurrence until that time, were now frequent as a natural result of inadequate maintenance.

Vast quantities of oil well equipment, pipes, casings and drilling machinery were transferred from ships to cars at Port Harford, or from the transfer platform at the Southern Pacific station in San Luis Obispo. Hence the new locomotives were a necessity and as fast as they arrived, they were immediately put to work. And none too soon, for No. 2, the old JOHN HARFORD blew up in its stall in the San Luis Obispo roundhouse while the watchman was out of the building having his midnight snack. Fortunately, nobody was hurt and the explosion did nothing more than wreck the locomotive and blow out a section of the roundhouse roof. By January 1905, four new locomotives had arrived and were on the job, while 35 tank cars provided three trains each way a day from Graciosa siding to Port Harford. Large storage tanks were by then finished at that point, and the flow from the wells accumulated there in orderly fashion.

So great was the activity around Graciosa Station at the foot of the canyon that it was decided to lay out a town a mile to the north, Superintendent Clark giving it the name of Orcutt, in honor of W. W. Orcutt, Chief Geologist for Union Oil Co. Streets were laid out and the town took shape rapidly, with stores, a small hotel and homes for the oilfield workers. The Southern Pacific, anxious to get in on this bonanza, helped finance a pipeline from their siding at Casmalia, the nearest

Orcutt oil field (*above*) in 1903 produced a gusher (*right*) which required a temporary dam (*top*) to stop flow of oil on ground. The same well in 1963 (*top, opposite page*) is now served by a nodding "horse's head" pump.

By 1913 oil from the Santa Maria valley kept Port San Luis busy loading tankers (*bottom*). — *Three top pictures: Santa Maria Historical Society; bottom: Roy Graves*

The oil boom brought great activity to San Luis Obispo station at train time (*above*); by 1935, Orcutt station lay sleepy, grass growing on the right of way. — *Middle: San Luis Obispo County Museum*

The first train from Santa Maria to Guadalupe *(top)* was hauled by Engine E-2. Until 1912 hourly passenger service was provided by Engine E-1 and combination coach No. 300 *(left)*. The locomotives were stored at San Luis Obispo *(below)* after electric service was abandoned. — *Bottom: Joe Moir*

point to the oilfields, to the Careaga and other small fields in the Los Alamos valley, taking some of the pressure off the Pacific Coast Ry. But not for long.

In October 1904, Union Oil brought in Hartnell #1 at 3000 feet, after many weeks of drilling. This well was supposed to have been drilled as close to the Pinal lease as possible, but a mistaken order caused the drilling to start at the edge of a steep hillside a short distance south, and when the well came in, it flowed an estimated 40,000 barrels the first day, tapering off to a mere 20,000 barrels daily when the initial pressure was relieved. Nicknamed the "Kaiser" by the drillers, this well was the first of many to be drilled nearby, and sixty years later it is still producing, though now on the pump. An earth dam across the canyon below the well saved the day again, while the narrow gauge carried away as much oil as possible. In fact, a newspaper comment of January 6, 1905 stated that the Pacific Coast Ry. had only managed to hold its own with the output of just that one well.

There was no stopping the drillers now. They were sitting on top of a bonanza and the Brookshire Co., which had drilled three unproductive wells, brought in their #4 a short distance from Hartnell #1, the roar of the gas being plainly heard in Santa Maria, eight miles away. Both Union and Standard were now rushing the work on pipelines to Port Harford, as the railroad could not possibly handle the business. Union Oil completed their pipeline first, but because their contract with the Pacific Coast Ry. had not yet run out, they left the pipeline unfinished for a number of weeks. Standard shipped dozens of tanks from their Kern County fields and confidently expected to be able to set them up on the hillsides above the Port. The Pacific Coast Ry. had a lease on some of the land on the bluffs, from the Marre Estate, and several tanks had been erected there, but when Standard Oil approached Gaspar Marre, administrator of the estate of his late father, Luigi, he asked such a high price for the right to cross the Marre land that Standard refused to pay it.

They then announced they had made a deal with Superintendent Clark of the Pacific Coast Ry. to lay their pipeline on the railroad right-of-way, and proceeded with its construction, as they had already reached Avila and were eager to finish the job and start the oil. But Gaspar Marre promptly got an injunction to stop the work and a shotgun to enforce it, calling attention to the fact that the land had been donated to the railroad in 1883 when the new line was built, *for railroad purposes only,* and that if it was used for any other purpose it was to revert back to the Marres. This stopped Standard in its tracks, but Union Oil got an injunction to stop the Marres from making any attempt to injure or destroy their pipeline, which crossed the Marre lands in several places, the Marres not having made any attempt to stop them at the time the pipeline was constructed. Union then made a conciliatory offer of $456,000 to buy from the Marre Estate its half-interest in the waterfront at Avila, the other half of which Union Oil already owned, twenty acres of shore land at Avila, ninety acres at Cave Landing, a right-of-way for both pipelines, and twenty acres along the bluffs at Port Harford for the tanks. The Marres accepted this offer, and John Harford, who had sold all this land to the Marres in 1883, hearing about it at his daughter's home in Oakland, died a few weeks later, perhaps of a broken heart thinking about the fortune he had missed.

As if to celebrate the end of the pipeline war, the Hotel Ramona, at the peak of its usefulness to the community, was completely destroyed by fire in the early morning hours of November 10, 1905. The hotel was jammed with 250 guests when the fire started in the kitchen, and within an hour the building was a heap of ashes. Fortunately, it was so far removed from other buildings that the hotel was the only victim of the fire, but it left San Luis Obispo without a resort hotel for over half a century, until the Madonna Inn came along a few years ago.

While the black gold around Santa Maria was commanding most of the attention, the sugar beet traffic was not escaping the eagle eye of Superintendent Clark. The Union Sugar Co. had leased a large portion of the Garey Ranch, east of Santa Maria, and a branch line was built from a junction two miles south of Santa Maria, eastward for 9½ miles to Garey Ranch, and then across the Santa Maria River to Suey Ranch house. A contract was let to C. P. Baird, electrical engineer and originator

A mixed train passes under the trees on its way to Avila.

Between Avila and Port San Luis the track was so close to the ocean as to be damaged by bad storms. — *Top: Vincent Canet; bottom left: Arthur Alter*

of the Baird Electrical Railway System, to electrify the entire line from the Suey Ranch across country to the sugar factory, a distance of 14 miles. The track work was completed April 15, 1906, and service by steam locomotives was provided temporarily until an electric locomotive could be constructed in the San Luis Obispo shops.

At the height of the oil hysteria, Superintendent Clark was authorized to build a locomotive repair shop in back of the roundhouse, which until then had doubled as a repair shop. In this new building, the first electric locomotive was assembled. To say that it was unique is an understatement. The chassis was built in the car shop, of oak timbers and flooring. Two General Electric traction motors were fitted to one four-wheel truck, and the other truck was the engine truck removed from the ill-fated 4-4-0 No. 2 which had blown itself into oblivion the year before. The control cab mounted on the center of the platform was the cab from the same steam locomotive. When completed, it was christened No. E-1, and after being tried out by Master Mechanic Ford, it was towed to Santa Maria and placed in service on the Betteravia-Suey line.

Santa Maria, which had become a booming city by this time began agitation for an electric railway to connect the city with the Southern Pacific at Guadalupe. The Pacific Coast Ry. agreed to provide this service, for in early 1906 they had built a branch four miles west from Santa Maria station to the Schuman Ranch and had added it to the electric lines. Two miles of main line between Santa Maria and the Suey-Betteravia line were also electrified. They would have completed the line to Guadalupe that same year, but the rails from Port Harford to San Luis, laid in 1876-1883 were wearing out, and the construction gang was moved to Port Harford. By the time they had rebuilt the 12 miles to San Luis, two years had passed.

Santa Maria was being literally smothered with oil discoveries during 1906 and 1907. Oil was struck in Cat Canyon to the east, the Associated Oil Co.'s drillers made a rich strike on the Miossi Ranch, and many a rancher who had been struggling thirty years earlier to raise enough wheat to make ends meet was now waxing rich from the oil royalties, while at the same time he farmed the land around the wells and pyramided his income.

In January of 1907, a cloudburst at Santa Maria washed out parts of the narrow gauge, but it did much greater damage to the Southern Pacific, marooning hundreds of passengers at San Luis Obispo where for lack of hotel accommodations they were forced to sit in the trains and wait until the Pacific Coast S. S. Co. could rush passenger steamers to Port Harford. In March, Tunnel #6 on the Cuesta grade caved in from end to end, and to rescue the hundreds of stranded passengers, the Pacific Coast S. S. Co. was asked to have their two largest and newest passenger ships diverted to Port Harford, where the Pacific Coast Ry. took the victims of this latest wrath of the Cuesta.

To provide through service, the Southern Pacific operated trains north from Los Angeles to San Luis, and south to Santa Margarita, while from the barns and backyards, all the old stage coaches were resurrected and put back in service, hauling passengers between the two railheads. This went on for over a month, and to quote the *Tribune*, "great difficulty was had with the horses, which had never been used to working in fours or sixes, and it was quite a sight to see these coaches going up the hill with the fractious horses held in line by veteran drivers brought back from other occupations, the fearful passengers peering out of the windows and wondering if they would ever reach their destination." The Southern Pacific hastily eliminated Tunnel #6 altogether by creating a deep cut in the mountain, and reopened the line on April 14th, 1907.

If the Southern Pacific had its troubles, the narrow gauge was not far behind. For several years, the State of California had been stressing the enforcement of a new law requiring all railroads in the State to have air brakes on all cars, and to equip these cars with automatic couplers, known to the trade as MCBs. The Pacific Coast Ry. had not done this, and so on October 19, 1907, Superintendent Clark appeared before the Grand Jury in Santa Barbara to answer various charges and citations against his railroad.

A State Inspector had stopped a mixed train leaving Santa Maria for Los Olivos, and found all

Old Engine No. 5 was equipped with link and pin couplers which the line was slow to abandon.

After sixty-five years, the Union Sugar Company factory was still in operation in 1963.

26 freight cars in the train equipped with link and pin couplers, and no air brakes. In addition, he found a boxcar loaded with dynamite in the middle of the train, so he slapped a fine of $100 per car for lack of automatic couplers and air brakes, and $500 for hauling dynamite in a passenger train, a total of $3200. This brought Superintendent Clark to Santa Barbara on the double, for the Grand Jury not only wanted to hear about the missing air brakes, but to air the complaints of farmers that the railroad was neglecting its grain hauling business. To quote Clark as he testified, " In one breath the newspapers attack us for neglecting the oil business, and in the next they state that we are

paying so much attention to the oil carrying that we fail to take care of the grain crop. We have along the line a total of eight no-agent stations, and if ranchers deliver the grain to any of these stations and fail to notify us by wire or letter, we can hardly be expected to deliver cars to that station the same day. We haul more oil in a month than the entire grain crop of one year, but we have *not* neglected our grain business." Clark went on to blame the Southern Pacific for most of the complaints, although how this could be is hard to see at this time. He stated that all the passenger coaches and locomotives were equipped with automatic couplers and air brakes, and that the freight cars would be so equipped as fast as they needed repairs.

Superintendent Clark weathered the storm due to his eloquence and the art of persuasiveness which was to take him to high places during his career. The fine was suspended, and five years passed before all the freight cars had air brakes. In early 1908, work was resumed on the Guadalupe electric extension, and when the narrow gauge tracks reached the main line of the Southern Pacific on the edge of Guadalupe, the shoe might be said to fit the other foot, for this time the Southern Pacific refused to allow the electric line to cross their tracks unless a tower was erected, and a watchman would be on duty 24 hours a day. When the contractor attempted to lay the narrow gauge rails right up to the Southern Pacific main line on each side, Southern Pacific trackmen ripped it up, and for weeks the electric line was stymied. In the meantime, the rails had been laid up Main Street across Broadway and for a few blocks east to Eben Hopkins Rooming House, which became the end of track for the interurban service. The argument with the Southern Pacific was settled peaceably in March 1908 by running the electric line parallel to the Southern Pacific tracks until opposite the Southern Pacific station, to which point the streetcar riders could walk on a boardwalk across the Southern Pacific main line. Guadalupe, which had expected to have a street railway down its main street was out in the cold, and the franchise they had granted was never used.

The first electric train through the streets of Santa Maria to Guadalupe made its run on April 17, 1909, and what a train it was! Hauled by Engine E-2, a new double-truck 4-motor steeple cab engine built at the San Luis Obispo shops, the cars consisted of three combination coaches, one of them the road's eldest, the Kimball car of 1875. After its first week, the E-2 went off to haul beets to Betteravia and the older E-1 usually hauling one combo, provided the interurban service. To eliminate the long haul for beets from the Schuman Ranch to Betteravia, a new three mile branch was opened in June 1909, from Betteravia Junction to the factory, and provided electric service for the beets from the Suey branch to the factory as well. The old steam line built in 1897 was then pulled up, and today has been completely forgotten except for occasional legal wrangles over ownership of the abandoned right-of-way.

Superintendent Clark became a Vice President of the company in 1910, and was also appointed a Vice President of Union Oil Co., devoting most of his time to the latter job. In later years he became Executive Vice President of Union Oil Co., retiring in 1935. J. H. Sims became the new Superintendent of the narrow gauge, and a choice anecdote about him is still told to this day around San Luis Obispo to the effect that as Sims was driving a visiting company official on an inspection of the line, they passed a building close to the track. When asked by the official if the building belonged to the company, Sims replied without looking, "If it's painted, it isn't ours!"

In Sim's first year, a new oil field was discovered east of Santa Maria near Cat Canyon, resulting in the extension of the Suey branch 1.6 miles to Sisquoc. The tank cars were put back to work full time, and since some had been dismantled and the flatcars assigned to other work, a request for more tanks from the oil companies had to be made. The year 1911 was literally a "stormy" one for Sims, for a cloudburst in March washed out the Santa Maria River trestle and tied up through traffic for a month. In addition, placing air brakes on old freight cars proved too much for them to stand, and in a matter of months, fifty of the flats and a number of boxcars had been wracked to pieces by air brake stresses. It was necessary to build forty new flats and ten new boxcars in the company shops, and to repair many others.

The "Armstrong" turntable at the San Luis Obispo round-house operated by muscle power. The three men turning No. 105 do not seem to be getting very effective help from the boys behind the tender. — *Below: Walter Thrall*

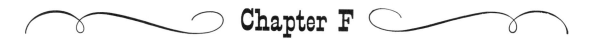

Chapter F

Competition and the Declining Years

THE GREATEST THREAT to the Pacific Coast Ry.'s freight traffic came in the summer of 1911, with the announcement that a refinery would be built at the new oilfields at Palmer, and a standard gauge railroad would be built by Santa Maria Oilfields of Calif., Inc. to connect the refinery with the Southern Pacific at Guadalupe. Chartered in July 1911, the Santa Maria Valley Railroad was given a right-of-way through Santa Maria just south of the business district, and construction was begun at once, the line being completed and in operation in November. As soon as the rival railroad was a certainty, Superintendent Sims announced that his company would immediately standard gauge their Guadalupe-Santa Maria-Sisquoc line and extend it to Palmer. He was spurred into action also because the new railroad's officials announced they would furnish passenger service from Santa Maria to Guadalupe with new Gasoline Motor Cars, in competition with the electric line. Apparently the management in Seattle, after scanning the cost sheets, reconsidered standard gauging their tracks, and nothing was ever done except to extend their Sisquoc branch to Palmer, the last piece of new construction on the Pacific Coast Railway.

The threat of passenger competition, and complaints from Santa Marians about the cumbersome locomotive and combination coach passing along Main Street brought about the ordering of a new steel center entrance interurban car from the Cincinnati Car Co., which was delivered early in 1912. It was ideal for the run, stopped the complaints of the locals, and squelched any idea the Santa Maria Valley R. R. may have had about passenger ser-

vice, for they confined their operations to freight service only.

The private automobile in 1912 was not yet a menace to passenger business on the narrow gauge, and in that year they had an all-time record of 62,319 passengers carried. Competition from buses began in 1913 and the passenger traffic went downhill in progressive steps until by 1922, only 3,547 were carried. The World War I years were very profitable freightwise, in spite of separation of the lumber and coal retail business from the railway operations in 1909, and the outright sale of the Pacific Coast S. S. Co. to H. F. Alexander in 1916. This left the parent company with the railroads in California and Washington, the coal mines, and investments in timber operations.

The earned surplus of the Pacific Coast Ry. reached its peak in 1921, when it was just under $250,000. The annual interest on the 6% bonds had also been paid, but none of them had ever been retired, and when the bonds came due on September 1, 1922, they were extended indefinitely, since they were wholly owned by the parent company. Bond interest was paid until 1931, by which time the surplus had been eaten up and a first class deficit of half a million was on the books. W. T. Masengill replaced Sims as Superintendent in 1924 and also sported the title of General Freight & Passenger Agent, but he had to fight a losing battle. In most of the years of his regime, operating expenses exceeded income; actually the surplus was gone when he took over, and never again was there a plus sign in the profit and loss column.

The rival railroad at Santa Maria, after several years of neglect on the part of its owners, was pur-

The center-entrance interurban car replaced Engine E-1 and coach on the Santa Maria-Guadalupe run, 1912. — *Marvin T. Maynard*

The Santa Maria Valley Railroad crossed Pacific Coast Railway narrow gauge tracks at Santa Maria. The old roadbed is still used for a mile north of this crossing, as a standard gauge industrial spur.

Engine No. 110, at the head of a gravel train, pauses for water in Santa Maria in the last years of the narrow gauge. — *Arthur Alter*

This antique switch stand at Santa Maria (*below*) survived to the end, even though the switches themselves had all been modernized in the early 1900s.

Santa Maria station in 1935 *(above)* served the narrow gauge Pacific Coast railway; in 1963 *(below)* standard gauge tracks of Santa Maria Valley Railroad pass the same building.

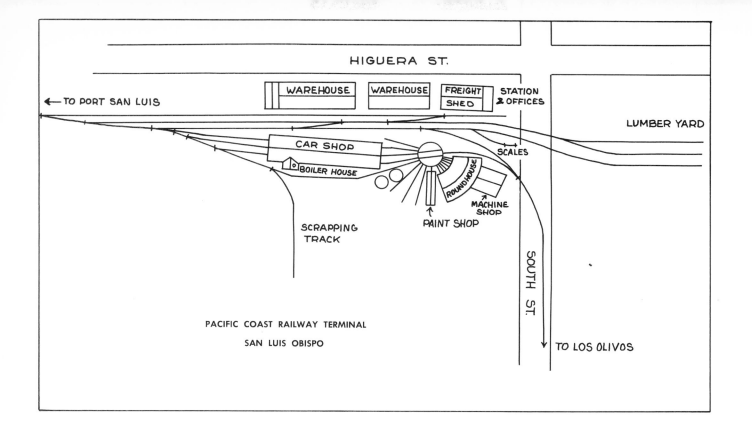

PACIFIC COAST RAILWAY TERMINAL
SAN LUIS OBISPO

Nerve center of the San Luis Obispo yards was the office and station which survived fire and age for many years. The line from Los Olivos approaches past a stub switch on one of the original 1875 stands *(top, left)*. The rear of the station is visible in the distance of the view of the yards *(bottom, left)* with the car shop at the right. — *Top, left: Allan Youell; center, left: Arthur Alter; bottom right: W. Young Louis*

Here are more views of San Luis Obispo yards: Tons of oil well equipment were unloaded *(top)* from Southern Pacific cars (right) and transferred to narrow gauge cars (left). The main line to Avila heads toward the hills *(center)*. Engine No. 105 leaves the station at the head of the daily freight for Los Alamos *(bottom).* — *Top: Allan Youell; bottom: R. B. Jackson*

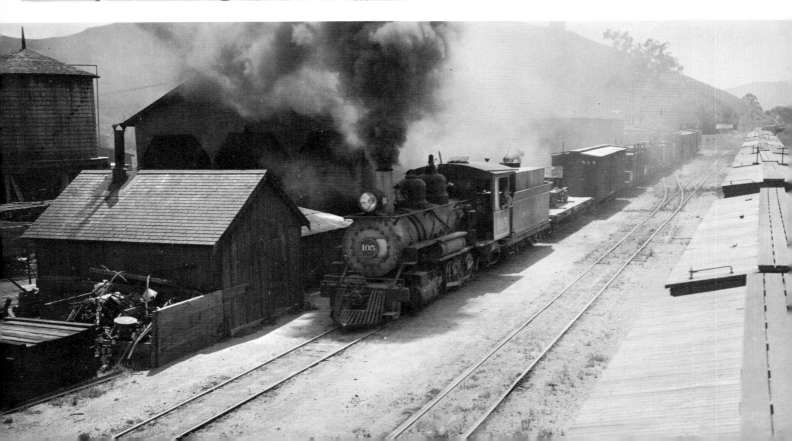

chased by G. Allan Hancock, who converted it into one of the country's finest and most prosperous short lines. With the Union Sugar Co., Captain Hancock conducted a campaign of education for the valley's ranchers, which resulted in crop rotation, with less sugar beets and more green vegetables which went to market in refrigerator cars, while the narrow gauge got none of the business. Due to other factors besides conversion of beet growing land to green produce, the sugar factory at Betteravia was shut down in 1927, ending beet hauling over the electric lines of the narrow gauge. The crash of 1929 and the depression which followed rendered the Guadalupe and Betteravia branches useless liabilities. The interurban trolley went first, in 1928, being replaced by buses, and the electric rolling stock was retired and stored in San Luis Obispo. The overhead wires were taken down and what little freight traffic was left to Guadalupe was handled by steam.

Amazingly enough, heavy demands by highway contractors for crushed rock and gravel from a pit near Sisquoc produced so much business that the road showed an operating profit in 1928 and 1929. This reduced the deficit enough to permit the purchase of two locomotives, ten boxcars, ten flats and two cabooses from the Nevada-California-Oregon R. R., which the Southern Pacific had just standard gauged. The two locomotives were heavier than the consolidations and more suited to handle the long gravel trains.

In 1930 the passenger train to Los Olivos from San Luis Obispo was reduced once more to a mixed train, with service twice a week, while on the other days the train turned around at Orcutt. In the fall of 1933, service was suspended between Los Olivos and Los Alamos, the improved highway into which the Sisquoc gravel had gone, having taken what little business there was left for the railroad. The line was not officially abandoned until 1936, when the tracks were taken up as far as Los Alamos. The passenger cars, except for a combination used on mixed trains were retired to dead storage in the car shop building at San Luis Obispo, awaiting possible use in motion pictures. In the early 1920s, several location companies came from Hollywood, the most notable one a picture with the hapless Fatty Arbuckle, and a special train was

used by this company for weeks at a time. In 1927 a picture named "Black Beauty" was filmed in the rolling country around Nipomo, and in the early days of talking pictures, the "Virginian" was made with railroad sequences involving the Pacific Coast Ry.

In 1935, Masengill's last year with the road, the coaches made their last appearance in the movies, in a picture titled "Diamond Jim Brady", produced by Universal Studios, and in the story was a sequence involving a railroad. Arrangements were made with Masengill to use several of the locomotives and practically all the passenger cars. During the week of May 15, 1935, San Luis Obispo was swarming with motion picture employees, with 500 costumed extras hired locally to appear in scenes made at Portuguese Flats, a short distance south of town. A set was constructed on both sides of the track, representing a small town in New York State in the early 1890s, and there Diamond Jim Brady, played by Edward Arnold, demonstrated the superiority of his steel passenger car over that of the wooden coaches then in use. Since the Pacific Coast Ry. owned no steel cars, it was necessary to fake one. Coach #103 had the tongue and groove wooden sides covered over with fibreboard, and the rivets were upholstery nails, so that from a distance it looked like a steel car. Coach #101, renumbered #105 for the picture, being in dilapidated condition anyway, had one end rebuilt with balsa wood, with the roof supports so weakened that when the scene was shot, the car would fly to pieces on impact.

Coach #103 was tied to the rails with cables and its front end reinforced with steel plates not seen by the camera. When the scene was shot, Engine No. 110 pushed the wooden coach head-on into the pseudo-steel coach, and of course the wooden coach was telescoped through half of its length. Additional drama was produced by the usual miniature process shots at the studio, which were intercut with the location shots. During four days the railroad was used from sunrise to sunset, and with Binnie Barnes as the feminine lead, Jean Arthur, Caesar Romero and George Sydney as the supporting cast, very little business was transacted in town, for most of the able bodied citizens were either working as extras or watching the free show.

During its last days the line appeared repeatedly in movies. A silent thriller was filmed near Los Olivos with Engine No. 108 sporting a phony balloon stack (*top, left*). Actor Edward Arnold, in the role of Diamond Jim Brady, stands on the running board of No. 106 at San Luis Obispo in 1935 (*below*). A spectacular scene in that film involved No. 110, lettered for the "New York Railroad" (*center, right*), and a steel coach which telescoped a wooden one (*bottom, left*), with fatal results to Coach No. 105 (*top, right*). — *All except top right: Universal Studios*

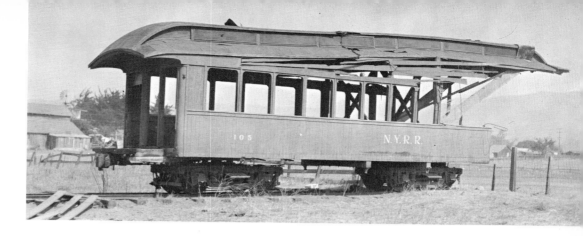

The picture, released in 1935 has been shown over television in the last few years. Coach #103 suffered little damage, but the hapless Coach #101 was a wreck, and was burned for scrap soon after.

In the fall of 1935, Masengill retired and the job of trying to hold the road together was taken over by Herbert C. Grundell, then assistant to Masengill, and Grundell was given the title of Manager, the only one to have this title since the days of J. Millard Fillmore. Grundell had been with the road since 1920, when after six years as a radio operator on various coastwise and trans-Pacific ships, among them many of the old Pacific Coast S. S. Co. veterans, he took on the job as telegraph operator and agent at Orcutt. In successive years he moved to Los Alamos and Santa Maria in the same capacity, then to San Luis Obispo. During all this time he had been studying law, and in 1931 he passed the California State Bar examinations. He continued with the narrow gauge, however, and stayed with it to the end.

While at Orcutt and Santa Maria, Grundell built an amateur radio transmitter and receiver, using the call letters 6DP. The writer, who had a "ham" radio station in Piedmont, California with the call 6XAO, used to work Grundell frequently. Neither of us ever dreamed that one day we would participate in a memorable excursion on the Pacific Coast Ry. In January 1937, the Southern Pacific had inaugurated the famous Daylight Limiteds between San Francisco and Los Angeles, and all railroad hobbyists and lovers of the iron horse were anxious to ride this train. In May of that year, the first special train operated for rail hobbyists west of the Rockies, and known throughout the world today as the "Railfan Excursion" had been run from San Francisco to Grass Valley, California and a ride on the Nevada County Narrow Gauge R. R. It was such a success that during that summer, the late Gilbert H. Kneiss, Chairman of the newly formed Pacific Coast Chapter of the Railway & Locomotive Historical Society, and your historian, the newly appointed Vice Chairman, discussed the possibility of an excursion on the Pacific Coast Ry. We decided that if the Southern Pacific would let us use three cars on the Daylight in each direction from San Francisco to San Luis Obispo, 150 people from each city could meet there, and a special on the Pacific Coast Ry. could haul us down to Port San Luis and back. We would then return to our respective cities on special trains provided by the Southern Pacific.

When I approached Alf Hammerstrom, special passenger agent of the Southern Pacific at Los Angeles, he said, "What! Tie up three coaches on the Daylights and let them run empty on half their trip — not on your life!" He added that San Francisco would never agree to it, even though the summer rush was over, but he said he would ask them and let me know. The answer was completely negative, but I phoned Gilbert Kneiss and his powers of persuasion were greater than the resistance of the Southern Pacific passenger officials. They agreed to let us have the combination car and the first two coaches at the head end of each train, or 150 seats, and no more. Manager Grundell was most cooperative, and not only provided the train and met the schedule, but set out all the other locomotives neatly in a row, separated by a few feet, with rods down, and in exactly the right spot for best lighting for pictures. Kneiss sold all 150 tickets long before the date set, and I sold all my allotment the same way, having to turn down at least 100 disappointed applicants. A few wise ones, however, drove up to San Luis Obispo, and quite a few local residents bought tickets for the narrow gauge ride only, for when we arrived at San Luis Obispo on October 10, 1937, a perfect fall day, there were quite a few "extras" waiting for us. Grundell had assembled a train which was reminiscent of the early days, for there were three coaches and a combination, the only ones left at that time, two gondolas fitted with benches and railings for safety, a side door caboose, and the old Santa Maria center door electric car trailed along on the end, minus window panes and doors, but jammed with passengers.

Hauled by Engine No. 106, all painted and beautifully cleaned, with Front Hampton at the throttle, our train stopped at the roundhouse for photos of the other locomotives, then with a motor caravan of dozens of local cars paralleling us to Avila, we went down to the wharf at Port San Luis and out to the end. After the engine had turned around at the land end of the wharf, by the ruins of the Hotel Marre which had burned several years

In 1938 railfans from Northern and Southern California arrived on Southern Pacific's ultramodern DAYLIGHT, transferring from the streamliner to the old narrow gauge cars at San Luis Obispo. Some stopped at the engine house to photograph the spare locomotives lined up in the sun. — *Top: Southern Pacific Co.; below: Roy B. Miller*

The excursion train, made up of a variety of equipment, took the railfans past San Luis Creek at Avila, along the shore of San Luis Obispo Bay, on to the old railroad pier at Port San Luis, where they saw the old warehouse. — *Above: Art Fleming; bottom, both pages: Southern Pacific Co.; top, opposite: Roy B. Miller*

earlier, it rearranged the consist so the electric car and caboose were on the rear, and away we went back to San Luis Obispo, with the caravan of autos still following us. At the Southern Pacific station in San Luis Obispo, two special trains were waiting, and promptly at 5:15 P.M., both trains pulled out in opposite directions, and for many of those who made this trip, it was their last ride on the Pacific Coast Ry. Certainly it was the last ride for the three coaches, for with the one remaining baggage car, they were sold to the White Pass & Yukon R. R. in Alaska, and were loaded aboard ship at Port San Luis early in 1938 for shipment to Skagway. All four cars are still in service, the three coaches having been converted into parlor cars and rebuilt as soon as they were received.

Application was made to the Interstate Commerce Commission on August 8, 1937 to abandon the Guadalupe and Betteravia branches, and this was promptly granted. The road was by then not earning expenses by a wide margin, and only a considerable amount of outside income from Port San Luis saved the road from abandonment then and there. Abandonment of the Sisquoc-Palmer branch was approved by the Interstate Commerce Commission in March 1940, and hearing that the rest of the line was apt to go at any time, a railfan club in Los Angeles called the Railroad Boosters organized one last railfan trip over the line, this time from San Luis Obispo to Santa Maria. A special train on the Southern Pacific left Los Angeles immediately after the *Daylight Limited* on October 20, 1940, loaded with over 300 people, arriving in San Luis Obispo about 1 P.M. There, Manager Grundell had lined up a train of open gondolas with benches and railings, and the road's last passenger car, Combination #106. Headed by the last of the consolidations, Engine No. 105, it looked for all the world like the first excursion train to Port Harford in 1876, which consisted of an engine, flatcars and the road's only coach.

The trip was made to Santa Maria in two hours, while the Southern Pacific special turned around and beat us to Santa Maria via Guadalupe and the Santa Maria Valley R. R. Two amusing incidents are well remembered by all who rode the narrow gauge that day, for when the train started across the Southern Pacific tracks at Hadley, the derail at the south end of the crossing was set against us, and no towerman was there to remove it. In the excitement of preparing for the crowd, the towerman had been forgotten, and because there were no narrow gauge trains on Sunday, he was taking his ease at home. Hastily summoned by loud and frequent blasts of No. 105's whistle, he set the derail and signal in our favor and we were off again after a twenty minute delay. Straining with nine heavily loaded cars on its tail, No. 105 pulled us around Horseshoe Bend and over the summit to Arroyo Grande. There it seemed as though the whole town was at the station to greet us — stretched across the track was a large rope, with a number of masked bandits holding each end, while other badmen fired off shotguns and pistols. The platform was filled with men and women in old time costumes, and as old No. 105 whistled off and started us on our way south, the people of Arroyo Grande cheered us on our way, just as their ancestors had welcomed the first train on almost exactly the same date in October 1881. At Santa Maria, we said goodbye to No. 105 and its genial crew, boarding our special train on the Santa Maria Valley for the run to Guadalupe, from whence the Southern Pacific gave us a fast ride home.

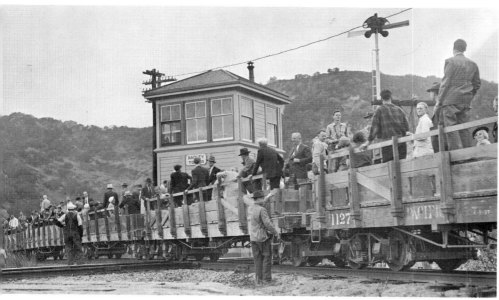

By 1940, with only one passenger coach left, railfans had to ride open gondolas on this excursion leaving San Luis Obispo *(above)* for Santa Maria. They were stalled for a time on Hadley Crossing, of the Southern Pacific tracks, until a derail switch could be unlocked *(left)*. Citizens of Arroyo Grande, dressed in old-time costumes, cheered the train. — *Bottom: Allan Youell*

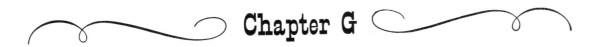

Chapter G

Liquidation

THE NARROW GAUGE had produced a million dollar deficit by the end of 1940. Its owners decided that they had had it. On April 21, 1941, application was made to the Interstate Commerce Commission to abandon everything south of San Luis Obispo, from Milepost 12 near Southern Pacific Junction. Although the Sisquoc branch abandonment had been approved a year previously, this branch was used to bring out carloads of gravel right up to the end. After suitable hearings the abandonment was approved on December 20, 1941 and in January 1942 all the rail was taken up and most of the equipment sold to Aaron Feher & Son of Los Angeles for use elsewhere or for scrap. Locomotive No. 111 was sold by Feher to the Oahu Ry. in Hawaii immediately after he purchased it, and the Navy bought all the serviceable boxcars for use at Pearl Harbor. These were repaired and repainted in San Luis Obispo and loaded aboard freighters at Port San Luis. It had been decided to continue the Port San Luis line but this soon proved impractical. The old San Luis Obispo & Santa Maria Valley thus became the beginning and the end, being sold to the Alphonzo E. Bell Corp. of Los Angeles on behalf of the Bell Oil Co. for $17,265, the road to be known as the Port San Luis Transportation Co.

Bell took over on February 28, 1942 and never operated so much as a handcar on the track, since no rolling stock went with the sale, and the line had been bought primarily to secure a piece of land along the shore near the wharf for oil storage tanks. A story has persisted through the years that the old electric car #3 was equipped with a gasoline motor and made several trips as Port San Luis Transportation Co. No. 4001. Ex-Manager Grun-

dell says this was not so, and has supplied the true story. In the last half of 1941, their Ford Inspection Car No. 4000 gave up the ghost and had to be retired. The best fishing in the Bay was off John Harford's old wharf, and as there was no highway leading to it, the Ford had been used by Grundell and several of the remaining employees for fishing trips on weekends. The old electric car was dragged out of the coach shed and Master Mechanic Mackie installed a 1928 Dodge truck motor in one end, linking it to an axle with a chain drive. Grundell had the car renumbered No. 4001, and with Mackie and others made a number of trips to the pier when the fish were biting. On their last trip, the car broke down on the way home and had to be towed in, which ended its last fling on the rails.

The demand for steel scrap in 1942 caused the War Production Board to ask Bell Oil for the rail on the Port San Luis line, arguing that since they had no rolling stock, they could not possibly use it. Going through the formality of asking the Interstate Commerce Commission's permission, Bell Oil was given the green light on October 19, 1942, selling the rail to the Dulien Steel Products Co. of Los Angeles. Engine No. 110 which was still for sale with no takers, was used to haul the rails to the Southern Pacific loading dock, and was thus the last locomotive to operate over the line. Port San Luis Transportation Co. fared very well in this deal, for though they showed a paper loss of $7,000 in their Interstate Commerce Commission application, they made a net profit of $6,000 on the sale of the rail at the prevailing sky-high wartime prices.

Manager Grundell took up law practice in San Luis Obispo as soon as his services with the Pacific

Coast Ry. ended, and distinguished himself through the years to such an extent that he was elected for two terms as District Attorney. To this day he checks in every night at seven with his short wave radio telephone, with the call W6JE, and enjoys a hobby in which he has been active for 43 years.

The Bell Oil Co. eventually sold the old wharf and the right-of-way of the railroad as far as the north end of Avila to Elton Tognazzini, who built a dirt road where the tracks had been and sold fishing rights for the pier at $1.00 per automobile, or 50c a head if you wanted a two mile walk. In the early 1950s the Port San Luis Harbor District was formed by the people of the County, and the State by legislative grant, gave the District the tidelands in San Luis Bay for the purpose of "Commerce and Navigation", but to reach the wharf, it was necessary to negotiate with Elton Tognazzini. Negotiations broke down, so the Harbor District started condemnation proceedings on Tognazzini's toll road and wharf. A jury heard the arguments, awarded the road to the Harbor District, but set a fair price at $707,000. The District could not pay such an outrageous sum, and abandoned the idea. Under the law, the defendant was entitled to his costs including legal fees, and the Court awarded

Bancroft, Avery & McAllister of San Francisco the sum of $125,000 fees plus $28,000 court costs. The District appealed this award, lost in District Court and the State Supreme Court turned down the appeal in May 1963. The Harbor District will thus have to pay the award from its own funds and by taxation, while Tognazzini still owns and operates the toll road.

John Harford's name came up a bit earlier when the land north of the San Luis Obispo station on which the lumber company had operated for nearly seventy years was to be sold. Harford had deeded the property to the San Luis Obispo & Santa Maria Valley R. R. for "Railroad Purposes Only," the land to revert back to him upon the discontinuance of the railroad. It was necessary to locate a Harford heir and have a quitclaim deed signed, and Harford's son was finally located in Seattle after a painstaking search and his signature obtained on the deed.

Though the Pacific Coast Ry. is now but a memory, fading from the thoughts of those living in the towns it served, it played a vital role in the development of the central California coast, and its history is a monument to the pioneers who built it, and to the generations of railroad men who ran it.

Gravel trains loaded at the Sisquoc pit until the last month of the railroad's operation. — *Arthur Alter*

A railroad's last days are melancholy. Service beyond Los Alamos ended in 1933, shortly after Engine No. 106 hauled this freight over the trestle near Los Olivos *(opposite, top)*. Activity that year at the Los Olivos terminal contrasts with the sleepy scene in 1935. Tracks, engine, and cars have gone *(opposite, center and bottom)*. A work train removes rails in 1942, between Avila and San Luis Obispo, hauled by Engine No. 110 *(above)*. In 1946, San Luis Obispo roundhouse stands forlorn, choked with weeds while cars, lacking both rails and buyers, languish in the sun nearby *(below)*. By 1963, excavation for the new road to Port San Luis having brought to light the old horse railroad tunnel, promised easier access by automobile to the old railroad wharf *(bottom, left)*, where the warehouse was now center for the local fishing industry. — *Top and center, left: Thomas Petersen; bottom, left: Al Phelps; above: Vincent Canet; below: Collection of Donald Duke*

Engine No. 110 *(top)*, just arriving on the road in 1928, proved too heavy for the track at Summit and went into the ditch. Engine No. 2 *(left)* went through a washed-out bridge near Santa Maria, 1890. Engine No. 105 *(bottom),* first time it used the Santa Maria gravel spur, 1904, was too heavy for the trestle and derailed. — *Top and middle: Author's Collection; bottom: Front Hampton*

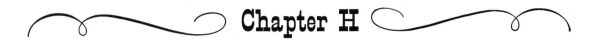

Chapter H

The Hazards of Narrow Gauge Railroading

N O RAILROAD HISTORY is complete without mentioning a few incidents which spiced up the news through the years, although frequently they meant losses to the railroad company. Fires were the biggest causes of losses through all the Pacific Coast Ry.'s history, for the wharf at Port Harford was twice destroyed by fire; first during the last week of December 1887 and second in the same week in 1915. In each case a number of freight cars were burned, but fortunately there was no loss of life.

Every railroad seems to have had at least one movie style emergency in which a train was used, and the Pacific Coast Ry. had one which is best described by the reporter of the San Luis Obispo *Tribune* on December 30, 1887. "Last Sunday morning the Christmas festivities were interrupted by the report that the wharves at Port Harford were entirely consumed by fire together with the Hotel Marre, pretty much all the rolling stock of the Pacific Coast Ry., and several hundred tons of freight on the said cars or in the warehouse. Our shippers mentally posted up to profit and loss in their ledgers, merchandise supposed to be in the vicinity and prepared for material changes in the yearly balance. Manager Fillmore received the word by messengers (the wires were down) and with Mr. Louis Marre and others largely interested, posted off to the scene of the disaster as fast as steam could carry them, experiencing great relief when at last the engine rushed around the curve at Avila and gave them a distant view of the scene. They found that the long rows of pilings apparently remained intact and that although the affair was bad enough, it had been greatly exaggerated. Arriving at the Port, it was found that the ware-

houses and offices had disappeared together with 275 feet of the outer wharf, along with 400 tons of grain and merchandise, and 11 freight cars. The Hotel Marre was intact, and only the heroic efforts of Mr. Gagliardo and his staff saved another dozen freight cars which were pushed to safety. The loss was $20,000, and the most probable cause of the fire was sparks from the stack of the steamer *Santa Cruz* which had departed shortly before the fire broke out."

Fire again destroyed the warehouse and outer half of the wharf on December 31, 1915, causing a loss of $30,000, but without the melodrama of the 1887 fire. The station and warehouse at Los Alamos burned in 1901 when several loaded boxcars went up in smoke. The great oil tank fire of 1908 at Orcutt was the most spectacular fire from the standpoint of smoke, and the loss to Union Oil exceeded $150,000. The railway lost some hundreds of feet of track and one tank car in the holocaust, but with typical resourcefulness, the railroad added extra coaches at San Luis Obispo and Arroyo Grande to the afternoon train from San Luis Obispo, and carried hundreds of sightseers right to the edge of the fire, at excursion rates, returning them home late in the evening when they had had their fill of watching Union Oil's storage facilities vanish in the flames.

Wrecks were surprisingly few, and a thorough search of all the newspapers through seventy years failed to come up with a single passenger casualty. This was undoubtedly due to the fact that the maximum permissible speed on long, straight tangents was 35 miles per hour, and the average was below 25 mph. Accidents there were, but com-

Engine No. 106 met its fiery end near Los Alamos when hit by a gasoline truck in 1938, less than a year after tak-

ing the Railfan Special to Port San Luis. — *Top: Collection of Front Hampton; bottom: Collection of Allan Youell*

pared with the fantastic series of wrecks and fatalities experienced by the Southern Pacific on their Coast line between Paso Robles and Santa Barbara between 1894 and 1904, the narrow gauge achieved near perfection in safety for both passengers and crew.

The first wreck, in which Engineer Masterman came out alive has already been detailed. The first crew fatality came on April 24, 1903, when a work train of flatcars and a passenger coach were descending the steep grade around Horseshoe Bend. The coach with 39 men aboard jumped the track and plunged down the bank. Only one man, Andrew Watson, was outside on the front platform,

and he was hurled under the coach and killed, while the others who were all inside crawled out the rear door after the dust had settled, with a few bruises and scratches their only injuries. Horseshoe Bend caused a number of derailments in its day, but the disappearance of brakeman Jack Stanton one night in September 1897, was pure comedy. When the up train stopped at Reeds, brakeman Stanton was missing and passengers in the last coach said he had been last seen standing on the rear platform. Backing up slowly while men stood on the steps of the last car with lanterns, they came upon a young lady waving a white cloth to flag them down. She disclosed that Stanton had been hurled off the platform when the car gave a sudden lurch, and landed in the bushes at the foot of the embankment, a bit scratched but able to walk to a nearby farmhouse for aid. Stanton decided he was not cut out for the rear brakeman's job, quit the narrow gauge and hired out as a switchman on the Southern Pacific at Los Angeles. Within a month he lost two fingers off his left hand by not getting out of the way soon enough. Recovering from this mishap, he returned to San Luis Obispo, got a job as a freight brakeman on the Pacific Coast Ry., and a year later lost the rest of the fingers on his left hand the same way, while coupling cars at the loading platform near the Southern Pacific station. That finished railroading for Stanton for all time.

In 1893, a freight train descending the grade at Horseshoe Bend broke into three sections, and there being no air brakes except on the engine, the two rear sections crashed into the head section, one at a time, telescoping two boxcars and strewing beans along the track for over a mile before the train was finally brought to a stop. Another time a boy on horseback was driving cattle across the track at the lower end of Horseshoe Bend, when a freight came down the hill, frightened the cattle, and caused a stampede onto a trestle, with the boy and his horse ahead of them. The cattle jumped down on each side of the low trestle and escaped, but the horse stumbled and fell, and only through heroic efforts of the train crew were they able to stop the train a few feet from the boy, who was not injured, nor was the horse.

Engine No. 2 went through a washed-out bridge a few miles south of Santa Maria one night in 1890, leaving the engine upside down at the foot of the bank, but with no serious injuries to either crew or passengers. Another time, Engine No. 101 created havoc right in front of the San Luis Obispo roundhouse in 1896, when it came downgrade from Southern Pacific Junction, rolled around the curve by the roundhouse, to find six freight cars still on the main line, left there but a moment before by a freight which had just arrived from Port Harford. Engineer Ed Dougherty had left part of his train at Steele's and had been sent in by Conductor Manderscheid to dispose of 15 flatcars in the San Luis Obispo yards before returning for the rest of the train. There being only one brakeman at the end of the string of flats, he could not set the brakes on enough of the cars when Dougherty whistled for brakes. No. 101 made kindling wood out of all six standing cars and their contents, throwing the shattered fragments right and left, while Fireman Rowan hit the dirt just before the crash. Dougherty stuck to his post and walked away from his engine unscathed. The entire work force spent all night clearing the tracks of debris and removing the damaged engine to the roundhouse for repairs.

The most spectacular accident, and the last of any importance on the railroad occurred August 10, 1938, when Engineer Front Hampton and his brother Stuart as fireman were on Engine No. 106, crossing the main highway a half mile west of Los Alamos in broad daylight, with a freight bound north to San Luis Obispo. Engineer Hampton always approached this crossing cautiously, blowing the engine's whistle frequently and ringing the bell, so on this occasion a Packard sedan with a lone occupant wisely stopped well short of the crossing and waited for the train to pass. But not so a tank truck loaded with 5000 gallons of gasoline, which was heading south on the highway at considerable speed, and when the driver saw the train and applied his brakes, they failed. Seeing he would be unable to stop, he jumped from the truck, which missed the sedan by inches and crashed into the side of the tender of the No. 106, derailing it and causing the engine and tender to turn over on their sides, pinning both enginemen in the cab. The gasoline caught fire immediately, and Fireman Stuart Hampton, freeing himself in the wrecked cab, managed to pull his brother Front to safety just in time to escape the oncoming flames, which burned the engine, tender and two loaded boxcars, as well as the tank truck and the sedan. The main highway was blocked for 24 hours, the power line was burned through, killing all the lights in the valley, and the loss was over $25,000. Manager Grundell said afterwards that only a miracle saved the two enginemen from certain death, but after chronicling the history of the Pacific Coast Ry. in detail, it would seem that the guardian angel who brought Engineer Masterman through the road's first big wreck was still working away at her job sixty years later.

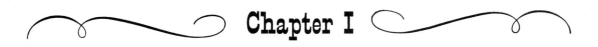

Chapter I

The Locomotives and the Rolling Stock of the Pacific Coast Railroad

Engine No. 4 was still a wood burner when this picture was taken at San Luis Obispo, 1884. By 1894 Engine No. 6 had been converted to coal.

PACIFIC COAST RAILWAY (3 ft. gauge)
Locomotives

No.	Type	Builder	Constr. No.	Date Blt.	Drivers	Cyls.	Total Weight	Boiler Pressure	Tractive Effort
1	2-4-2T	Baldwin	3771	8/1875	36	10x16	40000	125	4600
2	4-4-0	Baldwin	3968	8/1876	42	12x16	44000	130	6070
3	4-4-0	Grant	1410	4/1881	44	12x18	46000	140	7020
4	2-6-0	Grant	—	4/1881	36	15x18	48000	140	13400
5	2-6-0	Grant	—	4/1881	36	15x18	48000	140	13400
6	4-4-0	Baldwin	6921	8/1883	41	13x18	43000	140	8800
101	2-6-0	Baldwin	13732	9/1893	42	14x18	55640	140	10000
102	2-6-0	Grant	See No. 4						
103	2-6-0	Grant	See No. 5						
104	4-4-0	Grant	See No. 3						
105	2-8-0	Baldwin	23968	3/1904	36	16x20	73000	160	19340
106	2-8-0	Baldwin	24696	9/1904	36	16x20	73000	160	19340
107	2-8-0	Baldwin	24848	12/1904	36	16x20	73000	160	19340
108	2-8-0	Baldwin	25043	1/1905	36	16x20	73000	160	19340
109	2-8-0	Baldwin	27225	1/1906	36	16x20	73000	160	19340
110	4-6-0	Baldwin	34528	4/1910	44	16x20	89000	180	17800
111	4-6-0	Baldwin	37394	12/1911	44	16x20	89000	180	17800
120	2-4-2	Plymouth	—		Gasoline switcher bought 2nd hand. Acq. 1936				
1	4-4-0	Pac. Coast Ry. Shops		1907	Elect. - 2 GE 53 hp motors on one 4W Truck				
2	0-4-4-0	Pac. Coast Ry. Shops		1909	Elect. - Two 4W Trucks - 4 GE 53 hp motors				
3	Elect. Pass.	Cincinnati		1912	Equipped with Baldwin-West. trucks				
4000	2-2-0	Ford		1918	Inspection car made from Ford touring				
4001	Elect.	Cincinnati		1912	Old No. 3 equipped with Dodge truck motor				

Notes:

No. 1   Built as San Luis Obispo & Santa Maria Valley No. 1, named Avila. Equipped with 8-wheel tender 3/1882. Sold to Columbia & Puget Sound No. 5, 12/1883 and converted to an 0-6-0. Sold by them to Puget Sound Sawmill & Shingle Co. 1898.

No. 2   Built as San Luis Obispo & Santa Maria Valley No. 2, named John Harford. Blew up at San Luis Obispo in 1904. Scrapped.

No. 3   Rebuilt 1899 and renumbered No. 104.

No. 4   Rebuilt 1898 and renumbered No. 102.

No. 5   Rebuilt 1898 and renumbered No. 103.

No. 6   Ordered as replacement for No. 1. Shipped around the Horn; arrived 12/1883. Burned in Los Olivos Roundhouse fire 7/12/1896. Written off in 1900.

No. 101   Scrapped 1924.

No. 102   Scrapped 1/1912.

No. 103   Scrapped 3/1905.

No. 104   Scrapped 1/1912.

No. 105   Sold for scrap in 1943.

No. 106   Destroyed in fire August 10, 1938. Sold for scrap.

No. 107   Retired 1935. Used for spare parts. Lay derelict in San Luis Obispo until 1948, when the remains were scrapped.

No. 108   Retired 1935. Used for spare parts. All gone by 1940.

No. 109   Retired and sold for scrap in 1935.

No. 110   Ex Nevada-California-Oregon No. 10. Acq. 5/1928. Stored, for sale, at San Luis Obispo roundhouse until 1948 when it was cut up for scrap.

No. 111   Ex Nevada-California-Oregon No. 11. Acq. 5/1928. Sold through Aaron Feher Co. to Oahu Ry. No. 111, Hawaii, 1/1942. Scrapped at Honolulu in 1946.

Elect. No. 1   Pony trucks and cab from Engine No. 2 (steam). Scrapped 1938.

Elect. No. 2   Cab from No. 103. Scrapped 1938.

Elect. No. 3   Renumbered No. 4001 in 1941 and sold for scrap in 1942.

Plymouth No. 120   Built by the Fayte-Root-Heath Co., Plymouth, Ohio. Previous owners and date built unknown. Sold to Aaron Feher Co., Los Angeles 1/1942.

Engine No. 101 (above) still sported an unusual spark arrester on its stack, after conversion to oil burning.

Engine No. 102 (right), at Los Olivos, 1903, had also been converted to oil.

Engine No. 103 (left), on the wharf at Port Harford, with steam dome cover cannabalized from Engine No. 6.

Engine No. 105 (below), at San Luis Obispo, 1936, was the first of the consolidations ordered for the oil traffic.

Engine No. 106 was struck by a gasoline truck and burned in 1938.

Engine No. 107 backs on the San Luis turntable, 1931.

Engine No. 109 *(below)* stands at Southern Pacific station, San Luis Obispo, 1928. — *Above: Shirley Truitt; below: R. P. Middlebrook*

Engines No. 110 *(top)* and 111 *(above)* were similar; they were formerly Nevada-California-Oregon No. 10 and No. 11. Plymouth Diesel No. 120 *(left)*, shown at San Luis Obispo, 1938 had an unusual 2-4-2 wheel arrangement. — *Top: Allan Youell*

No.	Builder	Year Blt.	Type	Remarks
101	Carter	1882	Coach	Destroyed by fire in 1892
102	Carter	1882	Coach	Destroyed by fire in 1892
103	Carter	1882	Coach	Reblt. to comb. bagg.-pass. No. 301
104	Kimball	1875	Coach	Reblt. to comb. bagg.-pass. in 1909
105	Carter	1887	Coach	Destroyed by fire in 1892
106	Carter	1887	Coach	Reblt. to comb. bagg.-pass. in 1909
107	Carter	1887	Coach	Destroyed by fire in 1892
200	Carter	1887	Baggage	Burned for scrap in 1939
300	Carter	1887	Combo.	Partly destroyed in 1892 fire. Reblt. to combo. No. 107

Combination coach No. 300, ready to be burned for scrap, 1936.

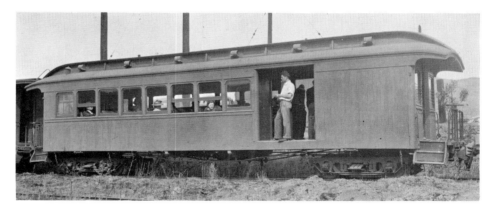

Combination coach No. 106 was the last coach to run on Pacific Coast Railway.

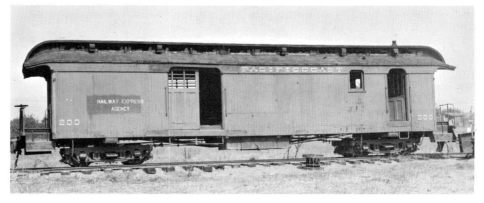

Baggage-Mail Car No. 200, surviving the fire of 1892, was finally burned for scrap after more than half a century of service.

PASSENGER CARS AFTER 1892 FIRE

101	J. Hammond	1893	Coach	Used as caboose after 1925. Wrecked for movie 5/1935. Burned for scrap in 1937.
102	J. Hammond	1893	Coach	Sold to White Pass & Yukon R.R. No. 258. Reblt. to Parlor car *Lake Kluahne*.
103	J. Hammond	1893	Coach	Sold to White Pass & Yukon R.R. No. 260 in 1938. Reblt. to Parlor car *Lake Tutshi*.
104	Kimball	1875	Coach	Reblt. to combo. for use on electric line 1909. Retired 1912.
105	J. Hammond	1893	Coach	Sold to White Pass & Yukon R.R. No. 105, 1938. Reblt. to Parlor car No. 262, *Lake Summit*.
106	Carter	1887	Coach	Reblt. to comb. bagg.-pass. 1909. Last car on road. Sold for scrap 1942.
107	Carter	1887	Combo.	Ex 1st 300. Reblt. to combo. in 1892 after fire. Retired in 1929 and burned for scrap.
200	Carter	1887	Baggage-Mail	Burned for scrap in 1939.
201	J. Hammond	1893	Baggage-Mail	Sold to White Pass & Yukon R.R. No. 207, 1938.
300	J. Hammond	1893	Combo.	Retired 1929. Burned for scrap 11/1936.
301	Carter	1882	Combo.	Ex 1st 103. Reblt. 1893 to combo. Retired 1929 and burned for scrap.

Coach 105 *(left and top, left)* was purchased by the White Pass & Yukon R.R., Alaska, and rebuilt as trim Parlor Car No. 262, LAKE SUMMIT *(above)*. Baggage Car No. 201 *(bottom, left)*, last of the J. Hammond series to operate in revenue service, was also shipped to Alaska, to emerge as W.P.&Y.R. No. 207 *(below)*, with cupola for use as a caboose. — *Left: R. B. Jackson; above and below: Carl E. Mulvihill*

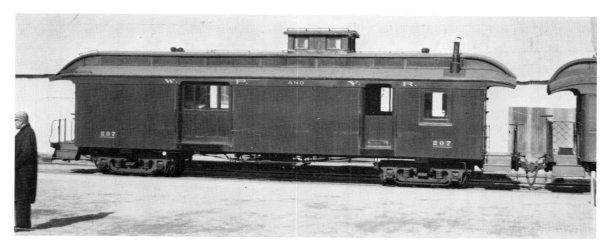

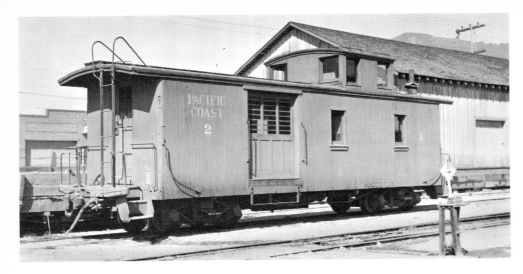

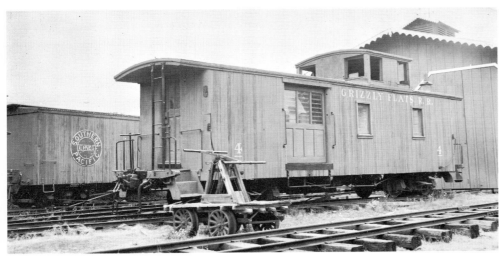

Caboose No. 2 *(top)*, when acquired from Nevada-California-Oregon, was equipped with a side door by Pacific Coast. In 1946 Ward Kimball purchased it for his Grizzly Flats R.R.. along with Boxcar No. 706 and a handcar *(middle)*. The caboose is being taken for a ride *(bottom)* on Grizzly Flats R.R. by a pair of Baldwin-built saddle tankers from Hawaii.

FREIGHT CARS

Numbers	Type	Builder	Year Blt.	Remarks
2 to 48, even Nos.	Box	Various	1875-1900	28 ft., Cap. 10T, Wt. 6T
400-418, even Nos.	Box	Various	1893-1900	28 ft., Cap. 12T, Wt. 6½T
700-718, even Nos.	Box	Seattle Sh.	1906	30 ft., Cap. 15T, Wt. 8T
800-818, even Nos.	Box	P. C. Ry.	1912	33 ft., Cap. 20T, Wt. 10T
1200-1248, even Nos.	Box	Pac. Car & Fdry.	1924	36½ ft., Cap. 30T, Wt. 12¼T
1500-1518, even Nos.	Box	Amer. Car & Fdry.	1900	30 ft., Cap. 25T, Wt. 11¾T
675-699, odd Nos.	Stock	Carter	1887	28½ ft., Cap. 12T, Wt. 7T
901-981, odd Nos.	Tank	P. C. Ry.	1902-10	33 ft., Cap. 30T, Wt. 9T (not incl. tank)
401-559, odd Nos.	Flat	Various	1875-99	28 ft., Cap. 10T, Wt. 4½T
601-679, odd Nos.	Flat	Various	1887-99	28 ft., Cap. 12T, Wt. 5T
701-749, odd Nos.	Flat	P. C. Ry.	1902	30 ft., Cap. 15T, Wt. 6¾T
751-765, odd Nos.	Flat	P. C. Ry.	1906	28 ft., Cap. 15T, Wt. 6½T
801-899, odd Nos.	Flat	Seattle Sh.	1907	30 ft., Cap. 20T, Wt. 6.3T
1001-1039, odd Nos.	Flat	P. C. Ry.	1910-12	33 ft., Cap. 20T, Wt. 7½T
1101-1239, odd Nos.	Flat	P. C. Ry.	1915-32	33 ft., Cap. 30T, Wt. 8½T
1501-1525, odd Nos.	Flat	Unknown	Unknown	30½ ft., Cap. 30T, Wt. 9T
1601-1613, odd Nos.	Flat	P. C. Ry.	1930-32	30½ ft., Cap. 30T, Wt. 9T
1041-1099, odd Nos.	Gondola	P. C. Ry.	1910-12	33 ft., Cap. 20T, Wt. 9T
1401-1439, odd Nos.	Gondola	P. C. Ry.	1919-30	33 ft., Cap. 20T, Wt. 9T
X-106, X-107	Tank	Unknown	Unknown	30 ft. See note
2 and 3	Caboose	Unknown	Unknown	29 ft. No. 2 equipped with side doors
18, 20, 34, 421	Tool cars	P. C. Ry.	Various	Reblt. from old cars
209, 300	Boarding cars	P. C. Ry.		Reblt. from old cars for B&B gang
453	Tower car	P. C. Ry.	1907	For elect. line maintenance

Notes:

Box cars 1500-1518, total 10 cars, built by Amer. Car & Fdry. Co. 1900 for Florence & Cripple Creek R.R.; sold to N-C-O in 1915; to P. C. Ry. in 1928.

Box cars 2-48 were built by Kimball, San Francisco 1876, Carter 1882, Holt Bros. 1883 and Pacific Coast Ry. shops.

Tank car capacity was 5700 gallons approx. Car No. 923 was 6676 gallons, and was the last tank car on the road. Tanks X-106 and X-107 were owned by Standard Oil Co., and were transferred to the Nevada County Narrow Gauge in 1934. The largest number of tank cars in service at any one time was 35.

Flat cars were frequently converted to low side gondolas as needed. At this writing, the only two freight cars remaining in California are Box No. 704 and Caboose No. 2, which were purchased by Ward Kimball in 1946 and are still in service on his Grizzly Flats R.R., at San Gabriel, California.

The last surviving tank car in 1937, at Arroyo Grande.

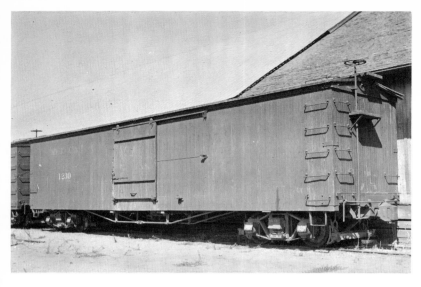

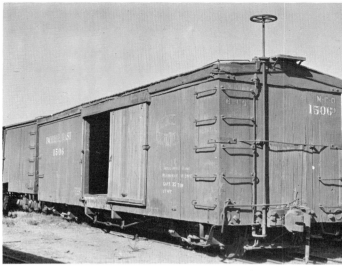

Largest boxcars *(top, left)* were the 1200 series, built at the Seattle shops in 1924. Boxcar No. 1506 *(top, right)*, began its career on the Florence & Cripple Creek R.R.,

Colorado, and did a stint on the Nevada-California-Oregon before coming to Pacific Coast in 1928.

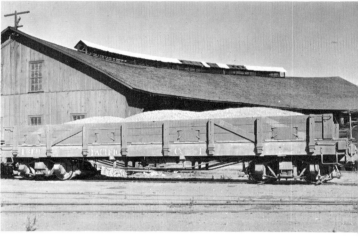

Boxcar No. 46 *(above, left)*, one of the original cars on Pacific Coast, built during the 1880s, at Los Alamos, 1936. Gondolas *(above. right)* loaded with gravel were biggest revenue producers during the 1930s. Short, 15-ton flats

(below, left) served the road for many years. The sway-backed 25-ton flat *(below, right)*, came to Pacific Coast from Nevada-California-Oregon.

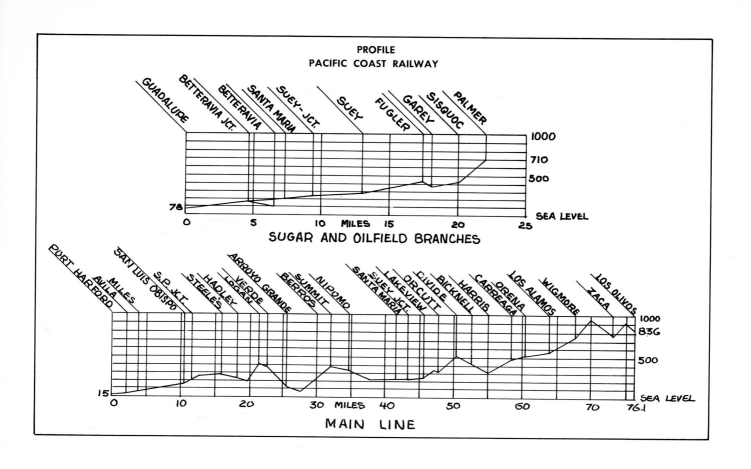

PROFILE
PACIFIC COAST RAILWAY

GUADALUPE · BETTERAVIA JCT. · BETTERAVIA · SANTA MARIA · SUEY-JCT. · SUEY · FUGLER · GAREY · SISQUOC · PALMER

1000 — 710 — 500 — SEA LEVEL

78

0   5   10   MILES   15   20   25

SUGAR AND OILFIELD BRANCHES

PORT HARFORD · AVILA · MILES · SAN LUIS OBISPO · S.P. JCT. · STEELE'S · HADLEY · LOGAN · VERDE · ARROYO GRANDE · BERROS · SUMMIT · NIPOMO · SANTA MARIA · SUEY JCT. · LAKEVIEW · ORCUTT · DIVIDE · BICKNELL · HARRIS · CARREAGA · ORENA · LOS ALAMOS · WIGMORE · ZACA · LOS OLIVOS

1000 — 83G — 500 — SEA LEVEL

15

0   10   20   30   MILES   40   50   60   70   76.1

MAIN LINE

PART II—THE STEAMSHIPS

Chapter J

The Pacific Coast Steamship Company

AT THE CLOSE of the Civil War in 1865, steamship service on the west coast from Panama to British Columbia was furnished by Pacific Mail Steamship Co., which had brought four side-wheel steamers around the Horn from the east coast to handle the mail contract from Panama City to all the principal seaports north of there. Mail from Europe and eastern United States ports was delivered to the Panama R. R. at Aspinwall, as the Atlantic port of the Isthmus was then called, and was delivered by railroad to the Pacific Mail steamers. In that same year three San Franciscans, Charles Goodall, his brother Edwin and Christopher Nelson bought the small steamer *Salinas* and several sailing vessels for trade along the west coast from Mexico to British Columbia. In 1867 they formed a company known as Goodall, Nelson & Perkins, Agents, with U. S. Senator George C. Perkins of California associated with the others in the business of coastwise trade. They soon became bitter rivals of Pacific Mail, and a feud between these two companies existed off and on for many years.

Goodall, Nelson & Perkins, or G. N. & P. for short, built up a fleet of small, wooden, propeller driven ships, none of them over 1000 tons gross, and almost all of them chartered from various small operators along the west coast. On the other hand, Pacific Mail used large side-wheel steamers averaging 1750 gross tons, some of them dating back to the early days of steam vessels, and they were expensive to operate and maintain unless filled to capacity on every run. The competition between these two firms in the 1873-74 period for the business at San Luis Obispo Bay has already

been related. This rate war covered the entire section from San Diego north to San Francisco and intermediate ports, and it came to an end during January, 1875. The Goodalls had acquired sufficient Pacific Mail stock to have a say in its management, and may have had, for a short time, complete control of that company. However, instead of taking it over, they reached an agreement with Pacific Mail to purchase from them six of their side-wheel steamers, their wharf facilities at various ports, and formed a new company to handle all traffic between San Diego and San Francisco, leaving Pacific Mail with the Central American business and the runs north of San Francisco.

A new company called the Goodall, Nelson & Perkins Steamship Co. was organized, in February 1875, and their new fleet, which included six Pacific Mail steamers, was as follows:

Ancon	*Donald*	*Mohongo*	*Salinas*
California	*Fideliter*	*Monterey*	*San Luis*
Constantine	*Gipsy*	*Orizaba*	*Senator*
Dakota	*Kalorama*	*Pacific*	*Ventura*

In addition, there were the sailing vessels *Sea Nymph* and *Mary Ellen*.

Within a year, Christopher Nelson retired from the firm, and the remaining partners then organized the Pacific Coast Steamship Co., which was officially in business on October 17, 1876. Service was furnished to approximately twenty ports along the California coast, and business was so good that the new company decided to give Pacific Mail some competition on the northern runs. Accordingly they paralleled Pacific Mail's run from Victoria, B. C. to San Francisco, with the usual rate war during which neither company made any prof-

it from their operation, and lost a great deal of money. After a year of this, another truce was signed, and a temporary peace reigned.

However, due to drought conditions in California in 1877, the lush crops being harvested in Oregon caused Pacific Coast S. S. Co. to enter the territory of the California-Oregon & Mexican S. S. Co. which had their steamers *Ajax, George W. Elder* and the *City of Chester* on the Portland-San Francisco route. There was no welcome mat for Goodall's company on this run either, and the ensuing rate war caused such heavy losses on both sides that a joint agreement between the two companies was signed within a year. Their ships were pooled on this run with rates stabilized, and both companies did well in the next few years.

In 1878, Goodall ordered two new iron steamships from Wm. Cramp & Sons in Philadelphia, and the first, the *State of California* was delivered in June 1879. The second vessel was the *Queen of the Pacific*, ordered in 1879 but not built until 1882. The *State of California* made a tremendous impression among coastal passenger agents, for it was the largest and most comfortable steamer in use on the coast in that year. As a result, the California-Oregon & Mexican S. S. Co. offered to buy out the Pacific Coast S. S. Co. at a sum calculated to swing the deal. Goodall and his partners were not swayed into hasty action by this offer, and it remained in abeyance for almost two years.

As if to thumb its nose at Pacific Mail in particular and all other rivals in general, Pacific Coast S. S. Co. again entered the fight for the Victoria, B. C. to San Francisco business, placing the former Pacific Mail steamer *Dakota* on this run. The *Dakota* was the largest side-wheeler of the fleet, weighing over 2000 gross tons, and it had accommodations for a large number of passengers. Fuel consumption of this ship was so great that in order to maintain a fast schedule and compete with Pacific Mail, operating costs were excessive. However, Pacific Mail gave up the fight in 1880, and with C. P. Huntington of Central Pacific Railroad fame at the helm, concentrated on the Central American field and eventually the trans-Pacific routes, never again to become a serious competitor of Goodall's company.

Branching out still farther north, Goodall then established service between Seattle and Alaska, operating the *California*, which they had bought for this service in 1881, renaming the ship *Eureka* since they already had a *State of California* in their fleet. With the *Eureka* were the *Ancon* and the *Idaho*, the latter two soon wrecked and lost, to be replaced by the new *Queen of the Pacific* and the *Mexico*.

This phenomenal growth of a purely local company attracted the attention of Henry Villard and in the latter part of 1881, Goodall, Perkins & Co. sold a controlling interest in the stock of the Pacific Coast S. S. Co. to Oregon Improvement Co., and with it went their control of the San Luis Obispo & Santa Maria Valley R. R. Goodall, Perkins & Co. was to remain as General Agents for the steamship company, responsible for operating the ships and soliciting traffic. Oregon Improvement then purchased a number of steamers which were turned over to Pacific Coast S. S. Co. to operate, and soon the company had the following routes:

San Francisco to San Diego and intermediate ports

San Francisco and Puget Sound ports

San Francisco and Portland, Oregon

San Francisco to Eureka and intermediate ports

San Francisco to Alaska and British Columbia

Oregon Improvement's control of the Columbia & Puget Sound and other railroads in the Seattle area, coal mines and lumber mills soon produced heavy traffic from Seattle southward as far as San Diego, and the company expanded steadily until the panic of 1893 brought about conditions which resulted in receivership for Oregon Improvement Co. In the reorganization, the newly formed Pacific Coast Company assumed control of all properties, with Goodall, Perkins & Co. continuing as agents at San Francisco. As of December 1, 1897, the Pacific Coast S. S. Co. owned and operated the following vessels:

Alexander Duncan	*Coos Bay*	*Santa Cruz*
Al-ki	*Gipsy*	*Santa Rosa*
Bonita	*Queen*	*State of California*

The Pacific Coast Co., successors to Oregon Improvement Co. owned the following vessels, all operated by the Pacific Coast S. S. Co.:

City of Topeka	*Pomona*
City of Puebla	*Seattle* (Barge)
Corona	*Senator* (Building)
Cottage City	*Umatilla*
Curacao	*Walla Walla*
Orizaba	*Willamette* (Collier)

The following are the names of the routes which Pacific Coast S. S. Co. served at that time:

CALIFORNIA NORTHERN — San Francisco to Humboldt Bay (Eureka, Arcata, etc.)

CALIFORNIA SOUTHERN — San Francisco, Port Harford, Santa Barbara, Port Los Angeles (near Santa Monica), Redondo and San Diego.

NARROW GAUGE ROUTE — San Francisco, Santa Cruz, Monterey, San Simeon, Cayucos, Port Harford, Lompoc, Gaviota, Santa Barbara, San Buenaventura (Ventura), Hueneme, San Pedro, Newport Landing.

MEXICAN — San Francisco, San Pedro, Ensenada, Magdalena Bay, San Jose del Cabo, Mazatlan, La Paz, Altata, Topolobampo, Guaymas, Santa Rosalia.

PUGET SOUND AND BRITISH COLUMBIA — San Francisco, Victoria, B.C., Port Townsend, Whatcom, Anacortes, Everett, Seattle, Tacoma.

SOUTHEASTERN (ALASKA) — Seattle and Tacoma via Victoria to Wrangell, Ketchikan, Juneau, Dyea, Skagway and other points north to Sitka.

The 1897 reorganization brought new life to the steamship company, and with J. D. Farrell as President, additional steamers were acquired, and particularly on the Alaska runs, business was on the increase. With discovery of gold in the Klondike, and the establishment of salmon canneries in Alaska, there was a heavy seasonal movement north in the spring and south in the fall. The new steamer *Spokane* was completed in 1902, and upgraded the Alaska service. That year marked the end of Goodall, Perkins & Co. as agents for Pacific Coast S. S. Co. After 35 years of activity in coastwise steamship service, during which they could be said to have been the pioneers and builders of this service, they requested to be relieved of the job, and on September 15, 1902, a new department was established in Seattle, taking over the duties as managers and agents for all shipping of the parent company.

The new management aggressively entered the Seattle-Bellingham route and purchased two stern-wheelers for that service, but all the other vessels remained on their regular runs. Some ships continued in the same pattern throughout their years, while others were shifted around as traffic demanded it. As was always the case with vessels operated along rocky and dangerous shores, there was a steady attrition of steamers, through fires at sea, running ashore in foggy weather, collisions in harbors, and just plain "old age". New steamers were built or purchased secondhand to keep up the fleet, and in the list which follows, every ship known to have been operated by Pacific Coast S. S. Co. or its predecessors is listed, with a brief history and description where the information is known.

In 1907, a number of changes were made which were to affect the whole operation of Pacific Coast S. S. Co. Passenger service on the so-called "Narrow Gauge" route was discontinued due to insufficient business, although the freighters continued to operate. Two large steamers, the *Governor*, and the *President* were built for a fast, long-distance run from Seattle, Victoria, San Francisco, Los Angeles, to San Diego. Easily the largest and fastest steamers then in use in coastwise trade, they introduced a new type of service and soon became very popular, especially during the summer season. In 1914 the steamer *Congress* was added to this group, in an effort to compete with the steamers *Yale* and *Harvard*, triple screw speedsters which had been brought around from the east coast by the Pacific Navigation Co. to provide fast overnight service between San Francisco and Los Angeles. Although slower than the *Yale* and *Harvard*, the *Congress* was noted for its comfortable staterooms, its fine cuisine and its freedom from vibration and rolling. Certainly anyone who ever occupied a stateroom near the stern of either the *Yale* or *Harvard* will remember the vibration of the propellers, as the ship raced through the night at better than 25 knots, and it is no wonder that the slower ships got their share of the business.

With the Panama-Pacific Exposition at San Francisco in 1915, the Pacific Coast S. S. Co. fleet as a whole made a record that year which became the high-water mark in coastwise steamer traffic for all time. This was to be the last year of the company's operation, however, for in 1916 all the passenger ships were sold to the Pacific-Alaska Navigation Co., known as the "Admiral Line". The charters for the *Yale* and *Harvard* were also purchased by the Admiral Line, which then changed its name to The Pacific Steamship Co. The steamer *Congress*, less than two years old, was not a part of this transfer, for on September 14, 1916 the ship caught fire while off Crescent City, California, and while the hull, engines and cargo holds were undamaged, the superstructure was destroyed and the passengers and most of the crew made it to shore safely in lifeboats. Some of the crew remained to extinguish the fire and operate the ship's engines while a tug steered it to drydock in Seattle harbor, where it was rebuilt at a cost of $2,000,000 by the China Mail S. S. Co., which bought the burned-out ship "as is". Renamed the *Nanking*, she operated for eight years in trans-Pacific service, until she was seized by the U. S. Government at San Francisco for carrying narcotics, and was sold at auction, returning to the Pacific S. S. Co. as the *Emma Alexander*.

The Pacific Coast S. S. Co.'s name did not die immediately, for the Pacific Coast Co. retained the trademarked name, and used its house flag on two freighters, the *Diamond Cement* and the *Eastern Guide* in the Alaska gypsum trade until 1938, when they liquidated the steamship company and allowed the name to fall into disuse.

Headed by H. F. Alexander, the Pacific Steamship Co. continued in coastwise service for 20 years, and one by one the familiar names of the ships which Goodall and associates made famous disappeared from view, as the steamers were either lost at sea, became obsolete or sold to make way for larger vessels. The *Governor* made the headlines in 1921 when it was rammed and sunk in Puget Sound in a dense fog, with the loss of a number of passengers, but most of the ships worked out their years without incident. The depression of the 1930s took its toll of coastwise shipping, the Southern Pacific introduced fast, overnight freight service between San Francisco and Los Angeles, cutting deeply into the freight business of the liners, but the labor unions precipitated a series of disastrous strikes beginning in 1934, marking the end of coastwise passenger service by sea. The 1934 strikes were bad enough, but in the summer of 1936 a worse strike was brewing, and one by one, the ships were tied up in early September and their crews laid off for good. On September 28, 1936, the old *Congress*, now the *Emma Alexander* tied up at San Francisco and marked the end of a service which had lasted over seventy years. Not that the *Congress* itself was finished, for in 1941 she was sold to a British company, became the *Empire Woodlark*, and when last heard from several years ago was still sailing the seven seas.

Today, the lucky few who ride the Matson liners *Mariposa* and *Monterey* between San Francisco and Los Angeles, en route to the South Seas, experience a little of the pleasure and relaxation from the cares of civilization which only a ship can provide. The California coast slips by a few miles to the east, the castle at San Simeon and the bluffs at Port San Luis stand out on a clear day in the light of sunset, and the dinner chimes sound through the corridors as the lights of Point Arguello flash in the distance, reminiscent of the days when this was the established way to travel, gone perhaps for always.

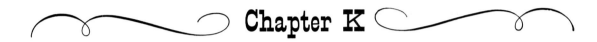

Chapter K

List of Steamships—1867-1916

STEAMSHIPS OF THE PACIFIC COAST S.S. CO.
AND ITS PREDECESSORS — 1867 to 1916

Alexander Duncan   Wood, propeller type, 371 tons. Built 1875 by Dickie Bros., San Francisco. Acquired by Pacific Coast S.S. Co. July 2, 1880. Converted to coal barge in 1902 and broken up in 1916. — *Roy D. Graves Collection*

Al-Ki   Wood, propeller type, 1259 tons. Built 1884 by New England Shipbuilding Co., Bath, Maine. for Ore. Impr. Co. Sold to Pacific Coast S.S. Co. Sold by them in April 1910. Wrecked on Point Augusta in 1917. — *Roy D. Graves Collection*

Ancon   Wood, side-wheel type, 1541 tons. Built 1867 by Jacob A. Westervelt & Co., New York, for Pacific Mail S.S. Co. Sold to Goodall, Nelson & Perkins February 15, 1875. To Pacific Coast S.S. Co. October 17, 1876. Wrecked at Loring, Alaska August 28, 1889. — *Roy D. Graves Collection*

Aurelia   Wood, propeller type, 424 tons. Built 1902 by Ross Shipbuilding Co., Prosper, Oregon. Purchased by Pacific Coast S.S. Co. 4/1/1916. To Admiral Line in 1916. Sold August 24, 1919 to American Merc. Bank of Peru. Destroyed by fire at Callao, Peru, May 1, 1920.

Bonita   Wood, propeller type, 521 tons. Built 1881 by Dickie Bros., San Francisco for Pacific Coast S.S. Co. Sold May 26, 1908 to Cia. Naviera del Pacifico, S.A., at Guaymas. Scrapped 1930. — *Roy D. Graves Collection*

California   Wood, side-wheel type, 1057 tons. Built 1848 by Wm. H. Webb, New York for Pacific Mail S.S. Co. Sold to Goodall, Nelson & Perkins in 1874. At the end of 1875 her engines were removed and she was sold to N. Richard as a sail-rigged ship. Wrecked near Pacasmayo, Peru, in December, 1894.

City of Chester   Iron, propeller type, 1106 tons. Built 1874 by John Roach & Sons, Chester, Pennsylvania. To Oregon S.S. Co. 1877, then to Oregon Railway & Navigation Co. Chartered by Pacific Coast S.S. Co. 1886. Sunk August 22, 1888 in collision with S.S. Oceanic at the Golden Gate. 16 casualties. — *Roy D. Graves Collection*

City of Puebla   Iron, propeller type, 2632 tons. Built for Ward-Havana line in 1881 by Wm. Cramp & Sons, Philadelphia. Sold to Ore. Impr. Co. 1883, then to Pacific Coast S.S. Co. December 1, 1897. To Admiral Line in 1916. To Harby S.S. Co., New York, 2/1/17. — *Roy D. Graves Collection*

City of Seattle   Steel, propeller type, 1411 tons. Built 1890 by Neafie & Levy, Philadelphia. Acq. by Pacific Coast S.S. Co. in 1910. To Admiral Line in 1916 and sold by them to east coast buyers.

City of Topeka   Iron, propeller type, 1057 tons. Built 1884 by John Roach & Sons, Chester, Pennsylvania, for Atcheson, Topeka & Santa Fe R.R. Acquired by Oregon Improvement Co. in 1891. To Pacific Coast S.S. Co. in 1897. Accidentally sank at wharf in Seattle September 11, 1904. Raised and rebuilt. Restored to service July 6, 1905. To Admiral Line in 1916. To Inter-Island Steam Navigation Co., Honolulu, 1921, renamed *Waimea*. Scrapped in 1933. — *Roy D. Graves Collection*

Columbia   Iron, propeller type, 1100 tons (approx.). Built 1880 by John Roach & Sons, Chester, Pennsylvania for the Oregon Railway & Navigation Co. Sold to Pacific Coast S.S. Co. and on July 21, 1907 sank in collision with steamer *San Pedro* near Shelter Cove. Casualties 64 passengers and 36 crew.

Congress   Steel, propeller type, 7793 tons. Built 1913 by New York Shipbuilding Corporation, Camden, New Jersey for Pacific Coast S.S. Co. Burned at sea September 14, 1916. Sold to China Mail S.S. Co. Rebuilt at Seattle and renamed *Nanking*. Acquired by Pacific S.S. Co. in 1923; renamed *Emma Alexander*. Retired 1936; sold 1941 to British interests, renamed *Empire Woodlark*.

— Below: Brian Thompson Collection

Constantine   Iron, propeller type, 796 tons. Built 1866 by C. Mitchell & Co., Newcastle, England. Acquired by Goodall, Nelson & Perkins February 11, 1875. To Pacific Coast S.S. Co. 10/17/1876. Scrapped 6/30/1887 at San Francisco.

Coos Bay   Wood, propeller type, 544 tons. Built 1884 by H. R. Reed, Marshfield, Oregon. Acquired by Pacific Coast S.S. Co. November 30, 1887. Went ashore near Ventura 1/28/1911. Refloated and repaired. Wrecked at Ventura pier by mountainous seas December 19, 1914. — *Roy D. Graves Collection*

Corona   Steel, propeller type, 1492 tons. Built 1888 by Neafie & Levy, Philadelphia to replace the *Ancon.* Owned by Oregon Improvement Co. then Pacific Coast Co. Wrecked in heavy weather on the breakwater at Humboldt Bay, March 1, 1907.
— *Roy D. Graves Collection*

Cottage City   Wood, propeller type, 1885 tons. Built 1890 by New England Shipbuilding Co., Bath, Maine for Oregon Improvement Co. To Pacific Coast Co. in 1897. Wrecked on Etolin Island, Alaska, 9/7/1902. Refloated and rebuilt. Lost at Cape Mudge, Alaska, January 25, 1911. — *Roy D. Graves Collection*

Curacao   Iron, propeller type, 1503 tons. Built 1895 by Wm. Cramp & Sons, Philadelphia for Oregon Improvement Co.; to Pacific Coast Co. 1897. Wrecked at Warm-chuck Inlet, Alaska 6/21/1913 and abandoned. Underwriters sold it to Vancouver Dredging & Salvage Co. and rebuilt. Resold to Pacific Coast S.S. Co. in 1916. To Admiral Line same year. To Alaska S.S. Co. 4/1/1932. To a Greek company in June 1940, and while en route from Grays Harbor to Hong Kong caught fire June 10, 1940, 104 miles northwest of the Columbia River; exploded and sank.

Dakota   Wood, side-wheel type, 2135 tons. Built 1865 by Henry Steers, Greenpoint, New York. Original name *Nicaragua*. Brought to the Pacific in 1873 for Webb's San Francisco-Australia line. To Pacific Mail S.S. Co. in 1873. To Goodall, Nelson & Perkins S.S. Co. 2/23/75. To Pacific Coast S.S. Co. 10/17/76. Retired account excessive fuel consumption and broken up August, 1886. — *Allan Yost Collection*

Delhi	Wood, propeller type, 968 tons. Built 1906 by Hall Brothers, Winslow, Washington for Pacific Coast Co. Used in Alaskan service. Wrecked in Sumner Strait, Alaska on 1/20/1915. — *Roy D. Graves Collection*
Donald	Wood, propeller type, 132 tons. Built 1862 in New York for Henry Ward. Named *Kiang Soo*. Sold to U.S. Navy 1863, renamed *U.S.S. Fuchsia*. Renamed *Donald*. Sold to Goodall & Nelson January, 1871. To Sen. Chris. Perkins August, 1872. To Goodall, Nelson & Perkins S.S. Co. 7/16/75; to Pacific Coast S.S. Co. 10/17/76. Retired at San Francisco 8/1889.
Eastern Oregon	Iron, twin screw propeller type, 883 tons. Built 1883 by John Roach & Sons, Chester, Pennsylvania for the builder, named *City of Palatka*. To Oregon Development Co. 1884; to Oregon Improvement Co. 1890. Destroyed by fire at Olympia, Washington 12/2/1891.

Eureka No. 1	Wood, propeller type, 689 tons. Built 1864 by Maxson & Fish, Mystic, Connecticut. Named *California*. Acquired by Pacific Coast S.S. Co. 9/28/91. Renamed *Eureka*. Scrapped at San Francisco in 1898. — *W. T. Miller Collection*
Eureka No. 2	Steel, propeller type, 2122 tons. Built 1899 by Cleveland Shipbuilding Corporation, Lorain, Ohio. Acquired by Pacific Coast S.S. Co. 1907. Sold Alaska S.S. Co. 2/18/16; renamed *Nizina*. Freight only.

Fideliter   Iron, propeller type, 175 tons. Built 1860 or 1861 in England as a sailing vessel for Russia. Arrived Victoria, B.C. 3/1/1862. Probably engined there. Acquired by Goodall, Nelson & Perkins 2/16/75; to Pacific Coast S.S. Co. 10/17/76. Went ashore at Cuffey's Cove, California 10/24/76. Loss 20 lives.

George W. Elder   Iron, propeller type, 1709 tons. Built 1874 by unknown yard. Owned by California-Oregon S.S. Co. Chartered to Pacific Coast S.S. Co. in 1888. To North Pacific S.S. Co. in 1897; sold by them in 1919. — *Roy D. Graves Collection*

Gipsy   Wood, propeller type, 239 tons. Built 1868 by Middlemas & Boole, San Francisco. Acquired by Goodall, Nelson & Perkins 1/25/75; to Pacific Coast S.S. Co. 10/17/76. Known as "Old Perpetual Motion." Wrecked on the rocks off Monterey September 27, 1905. — *Roy D. Graves Collection*

Governor	Steel, propeller type, twin screw, 5218 tons. Built 1907 by New York Shipbuilding Corporation, Camden, New Jersey for Pacific Coast Co. To Admiral Line in 1916. Sank in Puget Sound in collision with steamer *West Hartland* on April 1, 1921. — *Roy D. Graves Collection*
Homer	Wood, propeller type, 501 tons. Built 1891 by H. R. Reed Shipbuilding Co., Coquille, Oregon for C. H. Butler. Leased to Pacific Coast S.S. Co. 1898-1900. Acquired by Pacific Coast S.S. Co. in 1915. To Admiral Line in 1916. Sold 5/7/20 to D. Hanlon and refitted as salvage ship. Dismantled in 1929 and used as fishing barge. Scrapped 1937.
Idaho	Wood, propeller type, 1077 tons. Built 1866 by Geo. F. Patten at Bath, Maine for Anchor Line. Arrived in San Francisco 1867. Acquired Goodall, Nelson & Perkins 9/5/76; to Pacific Coast S.S. Co. 10/17/76. Wrecked on the rocks at Rosedale Reef near Victoria, B.C. 11/29/1889.
Kalorama	Wood, propeller type, 545 tons. Built in 1856 or 1858 on the east coast. Bought by U.S. Government during Civil War. Acquired by Goodall, Nelson & Perkins 2/24/75; to Pacific Coast S.S. Co. 10/17/76. Lost at sea March 30, 1877.
Los Angeles	Wood, propeller type, 495 tons. Built 1863 for U.S. Government. Acquired by Goodall, Nelson & Perkins 6/30/74; to Pacific Coast S.S. Co. 10/17/76. On April 21/94 struck submerged rock off Point Sur and sank.
Mainlander	Iron, propeller type, 484 tons. Built at Tacoma, Washington 1900. Acquired by Pacific Coast Co. 1902. Struck by tug *Sea Lion* in heavy fog off West Point in Puget Sound 10/24/04 and sank.
Meteor	Steel, propeller type, 2301 tons. Built 1901 by Craig Shipbuilding Co., Toledo, Ohio. Acquired by Pacific Coast Co. 1907. To Admiral Line in 1916 and sold to C. H. Sprague & Sons, Boston 11/20/16. Grounded on Block Island in fog 7/20/26. Total loss.
Miami	Steel, propeller type, 4900 tons. A collier. Acquired by Pacific Coast Co. 1899. Lost off Vancouver Island 1/25/1901.

Mexico
Wood, propeller type, 1797 tons. Built 1882 by Dickie Bros., San Francisco, for Oregon Railway & Navigation Co. Acquired by Oregon Improvement Co. 1888. Wrecked in dense fog on the rocks near Sitka, Alaska 8/4/1897.
— *Roy D. Graves Collection*

Mohongo
Iron, side-wheel type, 1331 tons. Built 1864 on the east coast for the U.S. Navy. To Pacific Mail S.S. Co. 1866; to Goodall, Nelson & Perkins in 1875; to Pacific Coast S.S. Co. 10/17/76. Scrapped at San Francisco 1881.

Montana
Wood, side-wheel type, 1004 tons. Built 1865 at Bath, Maine. Chartered by Goodall, Nelson & Perkins in 1871 and wrecked in the Gulf of California in December, 1874. Not owned by Goodall, Nelson & Perkins.
— *Roy D. Graves Collection*

Montara
Iron, propeller type, 2562 tons. Built 1881 by John Roach & Sons, Chester, Pennsylvania for Oregon Improvement Co. Named *Willamette*. To Pacific Coast S.S. Co. 1897. Named *Montara* 8/25/1902: To Admiral Line in 1916 and sold to eastern buyers. Wrecked off Nova Scotia 8/13/20. Was a collier.

Monterey
Wood, propeller type, 194 tons. Built 1869 by John W. Gates, San Francisco for Goodall, Nelson & Sudden. To Goodall, Nelson & Perkins 2/17/74; to Pacific Coast S.S. Co. 10/17/76. Lost at sea 8/19/1893.

| Newbern | Wood, propeller type, 943 tons. Built at Brooklyn, New York in mid-1860s for U.S. War Department by Pallion Bros. Acquired by Oregon Improvement Co. 7/14/88. Lost on rocks 6 miles west of Point Fermin 10/14/93. |

— *Roy D. Graves Collection*

| Newport | Wood, propeller type, 331 tons. Built by Dickie Bros., San Francisco, 1875, for Jas. McFadden. To Pacific Coast S.S. Co. 11/1/78. Sold to Pacific Steam Whaling Co. 6/1/92. Scrapped 12/1917. |

| Oregon | Iron, propeller type, 2335 tons. Built 1878 by John Roach & Son, Chester, Pennsylvania. Bought by Henry Villard for the Oregon Railway & Navigation and Oregon S.S. Co. Pooled with Pacific Coast S.S. steamers in San Francisco-Portland service. Sold to White Star S.S. Co. 8/21/1900; to Northwestern S.S. Co. 4/10/06; wrecked on rocks at Hinchinbrook Island, Alaska 9/13/06. |

| Orizaba No. 1 | Wood, side-wheel type, 1450 tons. Built 1854 by Jacob A. Westervelt & Co., New York for Nicaragua Transit Co. To Pacific Mail S.S. Co.; to Goodall, Nelson & Perkins 2/25/75; to Pacific Coast S.S. Co. 10/17/76. Scrapped at San Francisco 1897. — *W. T. Miller Collection* |

Orizaba No. 2   Iron, propeller type, 967 tons. Built 1883 by Harlan & Hollingsworth, Wilmington, Delaware, as the *Kate Carrol*. Acquired by Oregon Improvement Co. 1890 and renamed *Willamette Valley*. Name changed to *Orizaba* 2/12/95. Wrecked between St. Michaels and Nome, Alaska 9/17/1901.

Pacific   Wood, side-wheel type, 1003 tons. Built 9/1850 by Wm. H. Brown, New York. To Pacific Mail S.S. Co.; to Goodall, Nelson & Perkins 2/20/75. Sank November 4, 1875 in collision with sailing ship *Orpheus* off Cape Flattery, Washington.

Pomona   Steel, propeller type, 1264 tons. Built 1888 by Union Iron Works, San Francisco for Oregon Improvement Co. To Pacific Coast Co. 1897. Struck an uncharted rock off Ft. Ross, California 3/17/1908 and sank. — *Roy D. Graves Collection*

President   Steel, single propeller, 5218 tons. Built 1907 by New York Shipbuilding Corp., Camden, New Jersey, for Pacific Coast Co. To Admiral Line in 1916. Renamed *Dorothy Alexander*. Sold to Alaska S.S. Co. 1930. Renamed *Columbia*. Sold to Panamanian registry in 1944. — *Roy D. Graves Collection*

Queen of the Pacific	Iron, propeller type, 2727 tons. Built 1882 by Wm. Cramp & Sons, Philadelphia for the Pacific Coast S.S. Co. Sank off Port Harford May 1, 1888. Raised and repaired. Renamed *Queen* 5/23/90. Burned at sea 2/27/1904. Towed to San Francisco and rebuilt. Burned at sea again 1/24/14 and rebuilt at San Francisco. To Admiral Line in 1916. Scrapped at Osaka, Japan during 1935. *— Roy D. Graves Collection*
Ramona	Wood, propeller type, 1061 tons. Built 1902 by John W. Dickie, Alameda, California for Pacific Coast Co. Wrecked off the Spanish Islands in Alaska September 10, 1911.
Ravalli	Wood, propeller type, 998 tons. Built by Hans D. Bendixsen, Fairhaven, California. Acquired by Pacific Coast S.S. Co. in 1915. To Admiral Line, 1916.

Salinas	Wood, propeller type, 157 tons. Built by Jos. Ringat, San Francisco, for Robt. Sudden and associates. First ship leased by Goodall, Nelson & Perkins. To Goodall, Nelson & Perkins S.S. Co. 3/10/75; to Pacific Coast S.S. Co. 10/17/76. Scrapped at San Francisco 12/1889. — *W. T. Miller Collection*

San Luis	Wood, propeller type, 319 tons. Built 1864 by John Fardy Bros., Baltimore, Maryland as U.S. Revenue Cutter *Abraham Lincoln*. Acquired May 1874 by Goodall, Nelson & Perkins and renamed *San Luis*. To Goodall, Nelson & Perkins S.S. Co. 2/12/75; to Pacific Coast S.S. Co. 10/17/76. Sold to N. Bickard 5/15/80, stripped of machinery and converted to a barkentine. Lost at sea 3/14/1887.
San Vicente	Wood, propeller type, 246 tons. Built 1875 by Dickie Bros., San Francisco for Santa Cruz Lime Co. To Goodall, Nelson & Perkins 6/30/76; to Pacific Coast S.S. Co. 10/17/76; destroyed by fire off Pigeon Point, California 12/20/87. Twelve crew lost.
Santa Cruz	Wood, propeller type, 600 tons. Built 1868 by Jos. Ringat, San Francisco. Sold to Pacific Coast S.S. Co. 10/16/76. Sold to Puget Sound Salvage Co., Seattle, 1911. Converted to salvage ship. Destroyed by fire near Quillayute River, Washington 5/10/24.

Santa Rosa	Iron, propeller type, 2416 tons. Built 1884 by John Roach & Sons, Chester, Pennsylvania. Acquired by Oregon Improvement Co. 5/5/87; to Pacific Coast S.S. Co. 1897. Grounded July 7, 1911 north of Point Arguello, California and was a total loss. Three crew lost. — *Fitch Photo*
Sehome	Wood, stern-wheel type. Built in 1877 at The Dalles, Oregon as the *Mountain Queen*, for the Oregon Railway & Navigation Co. Rebuilt to side-wheel type, 692 tons gross, in 1889. To Pacific Coast Co. 11/6/02 for Seattle-Bellingham run. Sold to Monticello S.S. Co., San Francisco and rebuilt to twin-screw propeller type in 1908, using engines from an old destroyer. Sunk in collision with steamer *General Frisbie* in San Pablo Bay, December 14, 1918.

Goodall, Nelson & Perkins' S. S. "SENATOR,"
PLYING BETWEEN SAN FRANCISCO AND SOUTHERN COAST PORTS
HOUSEWORTH & CO. OHOTOGRAPHERS, 9 & 12 MONTGOMERY ST. SAN FRANCISCO

Senator No. 1 Wood, side-wheel type, 1012 tons. Built 1848 by Wm. H. Brown, New York. Early owners unknown. Came to the Pacific under Pacific Mail S.S. Co. flag. To Goodall, Nelson & Perkins 2/18/75; to Pacific Coast S.S. Co. 10/17/76. Sold to a New Zealand company in 1884 and converted in New Zealand to a coal barge.
— *Roy D. Graves Collection*

Senator No. 2 Steel, propeller type, 2409 tons. Built 1898 by the Union Iron Works, San Francisco for Pacific Coast Co. To Admiral Line in 1916. Renamed *Admiral Fiske* March 9, 1923. Sold to Japan for scrap in 1934. — *Roy D. Graves Collection*

Spokane   Steel, propeller type, 2036 tons. Built 1902 by Union Iron Works, San Francisco for Pacific Coast Co., Alaska run. Grounded in Seymour Narrows June 30, 1911 —2 lives lost. Refloated July 24, 1911 and rebuilt. To Admiral Line in 1916 and renamed *Admiral Rogers*. Scrapped in Japan in 1935. — *Roy D. Graves Collection*

State of California   Iron, propeller type, 2266 tons. Built 1879 by Wm. Cramp & Sons, Philadelphia, for Pacific Coast S.S. Co. In leaving Gambier Bay, Alaska 6/17/13 she struck an uncharted rock and sank, with 33 passengers and 7 crew lost.
— *Roy D. Graves Collection*

State of Washington   Wood, stern-wheel type, 605 tons. Built 1889 at Tacoma, Washington for Pacific Navigation Co. Acquired by Pacific Coast Co. 1902 for Puget Sound traffic. Sold June 12, 1905. Boiler exploded off Tongue Point June 23, 1920 and ship sank.

St. Paul	Iron, propeller type, 889 tons. Built 1875 by Wm. Cramp & Sons, Philadelphia, for Alaska Commercial Co., San Francisco. Sold to Chas. Goodall in 1893 and by him to Pacific Coast S.S. Co. in 1894. Wrecked 8/9/1896 on Point Joe, near Monterey. — *Roy D. Graves Collection*
Tampico	Steel, propeller type, 2133 tons. Built 1900 by Craig Shipbuilding Co., Toledo, Ohio, for Nicholson Transit Co., Michigan. Acquired by Pacific Coast Co. 1907. Beached at Seattle 5/18/11 account open sea valve. Raised and rebuilt. To Admiral Line, 1916.

Umatilla	Iron, propeller type, 3069 tons. Built 1881 by John Roach & Sons, Chester, Pennsylvania for Oregon Improvement Co. To Pacific Coast Co. 1897; to Admiral Line in 1916. Wrecked off Japanese Coast in 1918. — *Roy D. Graves Collection*

Valencia	Iron, propeller type, 1598 tons. Built 1882 by Wm. Cramp & Sons, Philadelphia, for Atlantic & Caribbean Navigation Co. To Pacific Steam Whaling Co. 1888; to Oregon Improvement Co. 1889; to Pacific Coast Co. 1897. On January 22, 1906 en route from San Francisco to Seattle, ran ashore on Vancouver Island in heavy weather at entrance to Straits of Juan de Fuca. 124 lives lost.
Vaquero	Wood, side-wheel type, 106 net tons. Launched September 1865 at the Allen shipyard in San Francisco. Operated on San Francisco Bay, 1865-1870, coastwise as far south as Newport 1870-1873, then on San Francisco Bay, 1873-1881. Acquired by Pacific Coast S.S. Co. 12/4/76 and retired 12/27/1881.
Ventura	Wood, propeller type, 775 tons. Built 1866 at Portsmouth, New Hampshire for U.S. Navy. Acquired by Goodall, Nelson & Perkins June 4, 1873. Wrecked off Santa Cruz April 20, 1875.
Victoria	Nothing is known about this vessel except that it was a collier and freighter acquired by Goodall, Nelson & Perkins in 1872 and operated between San Francisco and British Columbia. It was lost off Port Orford Reef in 1882 and presumably was a Pacific Coast S.S. Co. ship at that time.

Walla Walla	Iron, propeller type, 3069 tons. Built 1881 by John Roach & Sons, Chester, Pennsylvania for Oregon Improvement Co. To Pacific Coast S.S. Co. 3/2/98. Lost in collision with French sailing vessel *Max*, 9 miles off Cape Mendocino January 2, 1902, with loss of 16 passengers and 20 crew. — *Williamson's Marine Photo Shop*
Willamette	See *Montara*. Went aground 3/16/01 on Denman Island. Abandoned. Salvaged, rebuilt and resold to Pacific Coast S.S. Co. 1902.
Yaquina	Wood, propeller type, 356 tons. Built 1881 at Portland, Oregon. Acquired by Pacific Coast S.S. Co. 10/3/82. Wrecked by going ashore in fog at the bar at Port Hueneme, California 8/1897.

San Diego's wharf was equipped with a railroad to bring ships from deep water and connect with the California Southern R.R. (*below*) Steam dummies, including the CAPTAIN GOODALL (*above*) provided motive power. A horse-car (*top*) line carried passengers downtown. The steamer *Queen of the Pacific* is docked in the 1885 photograph (*below*); a 1902 picture (*above*) looks toward shore from the outer wharf. — *Top: R. B. Jackson Collection; above: R. P. Middlebrook Collection; bottom: Richard Dodge Collection*

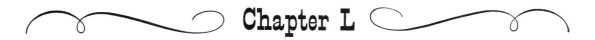

Chapter L

The Pacific Coast S. S. Company's Railroad at San Diego

THIS OBSCURE AND little known common carrier should be included in any story of the Pacific Coast Co. operations, as there was nothing else like it anywhere on the Pacific seaboard. In January 1875, at the time Goodall, Nelson & Perkins negotiated the purchase of Pacific Mail's steamers, the latter's wharf and shore facilities at San Diego were included in the transaction. This wharf had been built by Alonzo E. Horton in 1869 at the foot of 5th Street, out from shore over the mud flats to deep water 1500 feet into San Diego Bay. In 1872 Pacific Mail bought the wharf from Horton and equipped it with a narrow gauge railroad of the same type used by Peoples Wharf at San Luis Bay. On 20 lb. rail, horse-drawn cars handled the freight, and it is believed there was at least one passenger coach used to save the passengers a quarter-mile walk from ship to shore. A newspaper "wag" in 1873 reported that the "engine" on the railway track of the Pacific Mail S. S. Co.'s wharf ran off the track last Thursday near the shore, and was not found for two days. It was a horse.

Known as the San Diego Wharf, the Pacific Coast S. S. Co. used it without extensive changes until 1881, at which time it was decided to widen the railroad to standard gauge and provide connection with the California Southern R. R., then under construction. The wharf was lowered slightly to conform with the level of the railroad on shore, the track was replaced with heavier rail, and a spur from the main track which ran from shipside to the station on shore branched off midway to a direct connection with the California Southern. Over this spur, freight cars could be brought to the outer end of the wharf, but since California Southern's locomotives were too heavy for the piling, and the steamship company wished to control the operation anyway, two small steam dummy locomotives were purchased from the National Iron Works in San Francisco and brought down to San Diego in June, 1882. Open passenger cars hauled by these dummies shuttled back and forth from station to shipside at sailing or arrival time, or switched freight cars as needed. The first two locomotives were named CAPTAIN GOODALL and McKINLEY, the latter not Wm. McKinley, for in 1882 the man who later became President was a Congressman from Ohio and little known on the coast.

Business increased enough to require a third locomotive in 1888, also built by National Iron Works in San Francisco to the same design as the others, and named SENATOR PERKINS. In 1909 the CAPTAIN GOODALL was retired and no doubt used to supply parts for the other two, being replaced by a new Alco-Dickson 0-4-0T which while heavier than the dummies, was still a very small locomotive. In 1913 another Alco saddle-tanker by Rogers arrived, and the two remaining dummies were retired.

The rail operations on this wharf were discontinued in 1919, for the Bay had been filled in extensively, the new Broadway pier taking the place of the old wharf, which was abandoned, and new fill completely obliterated it. The San Diego & Arizona Ry. purchased the spur tracks, the locomotives were sold, and thus ended one of the West's shortest shortlines.

LOCOMOTIVES OF THE PACIFIC COAST S. S. CO. R. R. AT SAN DIEGO

No.		Type	Builder	Date	Remarks
1	0-4-0	Dummy	National Iron Works, S.F. (Marschutz & Cantrell)	1882	Named CAPTAIN GOODALL. Retired 1907.
2	0-4-0	Dummy	National Iron Works, S.F.	1882	Named McKINLEY. Retired 1913.
3	0-4-0	Dummy	National Iron Works, S.F.	1888	Named SENATOR PERKINS. Retired 1912.
2nd 1	0-4-0T	—	Alco-Dickson No. 45556	7/1908	Sold to Fontana Hog Farm 1919. Named SAN DIEGO.
2nd 2	0-4-0T	—	Alco-Rogers No. 46526	9/1909	Blt. for Alco stock and sold to P.C. S.S. Co. 7/1913. Sold 1919.

Motive power for the railroad on the San Diego wharf was provided by the five engines shown on these two pages. First came the CAPTAIN GOODALL shown, about 1890, at the head of a festively decorated four-car train (bottom) and with it the McKINLEY, shown unnamed (opposite, bottom) with the SENATOR PERKINS, a few years newer, in 1913, when both were awaiting scrapping. A dummy pauses (top) in a prosaic job while three men and a dog pose. The dummies were succeeded by the saddle-tank engines (opposite, top, and below); their diminutive size can be gauged by the boxcar which so dwarfs the second No. 1. — Bottom, both pages: R. P. Middlebrook Collection

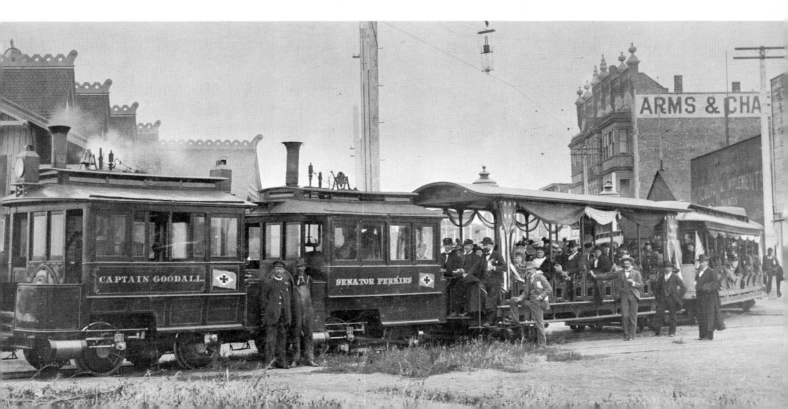

Seattle & Walla Walla Engine No. 1 is at the head of an excursion train to the race track. The size of little Engine No. 2 is suggested by the men posing with it on the turntable. — *Above: Homer G. Benton Collection; below: D. H. Roberts Collection*

PART III—THE PACIFIC COAST COMPANY IN WASHINGTON

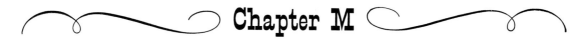

Chapter M

The Railroads

WHEN JOHN HARFORD was breaking in his horse railroad in 1873, and Charles Goodall and partners were giving Pacific Mail a rough time, the townspeople of Seattle in Washington Territory were in an uproar over the announcement that the Northern Pacific R. R., then completed from Tacoma southward for 105 miles to Kalama, on the Columbia River, would terminate at Tacoma.

This idea did not sit well with the citizens of Seattle, who had ambitions to make their town Puget Sound's main seaport and transcontinental railroad terminal. They petitioned Congress in 1873 for a land grant enabling them to build a railroad from Seattle through Snoqualmie Pass to Wallula, where it would connect with the Walla Walla & Columbia River R. R., a 3 ft. gauge line then under construction. The Northern Pacific had already completed a large segment of railroad from Duluth, Minnesota to Bismarck in Dakota Territory, and as their plans called for extending the railroad westward to the Columbia River at Wallula, a railroad from Seattle to Wallula would guarantee Seattle a through line to the east.

Seattle failed to obtain the grant, however, and decided to build a railroad by volunteer labor. Organizing the Seattle & Walla Walla Railroad & Transportation Co. July 6, 1873, they began construction of a 3 ft. gauge railroad at Steele's Landing on the Duwamish River, nine miles from Seattle on May 1, 1874. Viewed in retrospect, the selection of narrow gauge for their railroad was a mistake, but it was cheaper to build, and money was tight due to the panic of 1873. By mid-1875 they had graded the line a short distance towards Renton, and nine miles down-river to Seattle, but

had laid no rails. The Renton Coal Co. built two miles of light track from their mines near Renton, connecting with the Seattle & Walla Walla's grade, and donated this section in the interest of seeing the line finished as soon as possible. It was February 1877 before the Railroad was completed from Renton to Seattle, and by hauling coal the road was soon a paying one though it was doing nothing to settle the feud between Seattle and Tacoma. The Northern Pacific had gone into receivership in 1875, leaving the Tacoma-Kalama section an unprofitable orphan, while Seattle's railroad was solvent. Another locomotive was acquired by the latter in 1877, and in 1878, an agreement with the Seattle Coal & Transportation Co. was made whereby the latter furnished the coal and the Seattle & Walla Walla the transportation of it to Seattle.

Actually the first railroad in the Puget Sound area, Seattle Coal Co. was organized in 1870 to bring coal by mule or horse-drawn tram and flatboats from coal mines at Newcastle to Seattle. From the mines, the cars moved the coal down an inclined plane to Lake Washington, where the cars were ferried to Union Bay. Another tram brought the cars to Lake Union, where barges ferried them to a third railroad section at the south end of the lake, and from there the tram brought the coal to bunkers in Seattle. The gauge was six feet and the rails were strap iron, bolted to logs.

In 1872, after a group of San Franciscans had inspected the properties and decided they had great potential value, the company was reincorporated as the Seattle Coal & Transportation Co., with W. B. Cummings as President and S. Dinsmore as

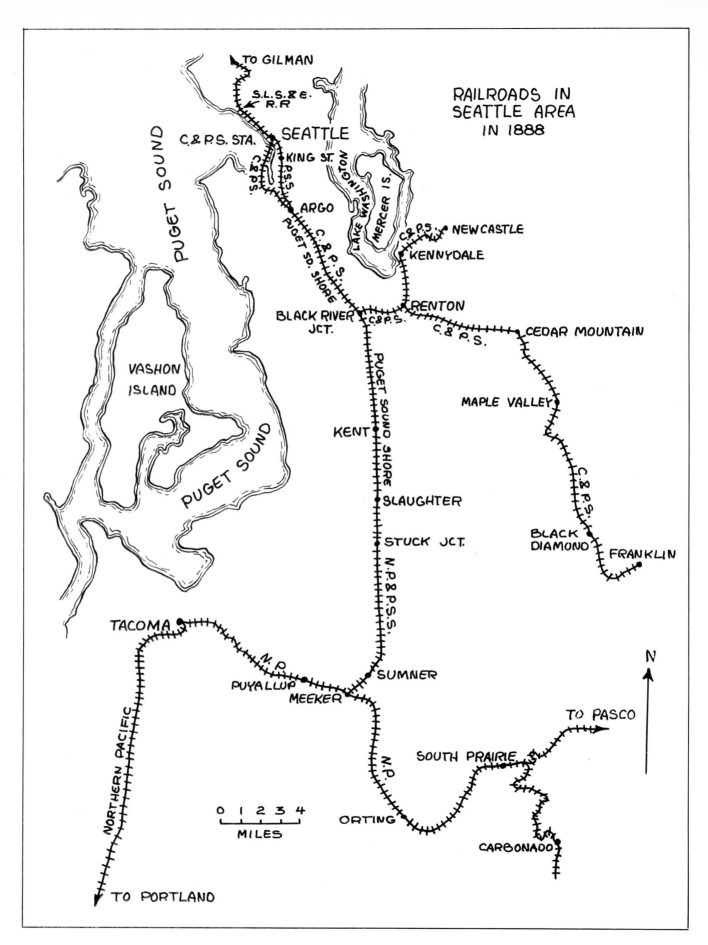

RAILROADS IN
SEATTLE AREA
IN 1888

TO GILMAN

S.L.S.&E.
R.R.

PUGET SOUND

C.& P.S. STA.

SEATTLE

C.& P.S.

C.& P.S.S.

KING ST.

ARGO

C.& P.S.

PUGET SD. SHORE

LAKE WASHINGTON

MERCER IS.

C.& P.S.

NEWCASTLE

KENNYDALE

RENTON

BLACK RIVER
JCT.

C.& P.S.

C.& P.S.

CEDAR MOUNTAIN

PUGET SOUND SHORE

KENT

MAPLE VALLEY

VASHON
ISLAND

PUGET SOUND

SLAUGHTER

STUCK JCT.

N.P.& P.S.S.

C.& P.S.

BLACK
DIAMOND

FRANKLIN

TACOMA

N.P.

SUMNER

PUYALLUP

MEEKER

N

NORTHERN PACIFIC

N.P.

TO PASCO

SOUTH PRAIRIE

0 1 2 3 4
MILES

ORTING

CARBONADO

TO PORTLAND

Manager. Dinsmore was given the job of improving the railroad, and the mines at Newcastle. A small saddle-tank locomotive called the ANT was brought up from San Francisco, replacing the mules on the Seattle-Lake Union section. The gauge was narrowed to three feet, with iron rails replacing the wood and strap iron, and in March 1872 the first passenger train ever to leave Seattle was hauled by the ANT, it being the usual open-air excursion with the passengers seated in coal cars. Before this event, Dinsmore had already narrowed the gauge on the other sections and improved the roadbed, so in 1874 a new Baldwin saddle-tank 0-6-0 was purchased to replace the horses on the Seattle and Lake Union sections and in 1875 he bought another Baldwin of the same type. This coal operation continued until 1878, when the Seattle & Walla Walla, having extended its line from Renton to Newcastle the previous year, contracted with the Seattle Coal & Transportation Co. to haul all its coal, and took over the locomotives and rolling stock of the portage railroad, which at best was a slow and laborious operation.

In 1880, Henry Villard came on the western scene as the new President of the Oregon Ry. & Navigation Co., taking over the Presidency of the Oregon & California R. R. a few months later, and joining the Board of Directors of the Northern Pacific. Now Villard was a man of dynamic personality and a man of action as well, for he had had a long and distinguished career in other fields. Born in Germany as Henry Hilgard, he immigrated to the United States in 1853 and changed his name to Villard. As a newspaper correspondent for the Chicago *Tribune*, he became famous for his reporting of the Civil War as seen from the Northern side. In 1873 he was selected by a large group of German owners of Northern Pacific bonds to represent them in the United States, and became vitally interested in that road. On September 25, 1880, Frederick Billings was replaced by Villard as President of the Northern Pacific, at a directors' meeting in New York, and this placed Villard at the helm of three railroads, all with interests in the great Northwest.

His first move was to organize two holding companies, the Oregon & Transcontinental Co., to harmonize the relations between the Oregon Ry. & Nav. Co., and the Northern Pacific; and the Oregon Improvement Co., a subsidiary of the Oregon Ry. & Nav. Co., to develop coastwise trade from Puget Sound ports to California. Purchasing the Seattle & Walla Walla R. R. & Transp. Co. to insure a supply of coal, Villard combined it with the Seattle Coal & Transp. Co., reincorporating as the Columbia & Puget Sound R. R. on November 26, 1880, with a capital stock of $575,000. Reaching down into California, Villard gained control of the Pacific Coast S. S. Co., and through it the railroad of the same name.

Villard visited Seattle in 1881 and told its businessmen he believed that Seattle should be the terminal of the Northern Pacific instead of Tacoma. He agreed with them that Seattle should have a rail connection with Tacoma as soon as possible, and to gain this end, his Oregon & Transcontinental Co. organized the Puget Sound Shore R. R. on August 19, 1882. The nearest point on the Columbia & Puget Sound to Tacoma was at Black River, and so a standard gauge track was laid south from there for a distance of 14 miles, where it met a seven mile extension built by the Northern Pacific from its Cascade branch, near the station of Meeker. The meeting point of these two lines was near the present town of Auburn and was called Stuck Jct. To connect these sections with Seattle, a third rail was then laid on the Columbia & Puget Sound roadbed from Black River to Argo, with a new standard gauge track built from Argo to a new station in Seattle. Using Northern Pacific rolling stock, trains began to run through from Tacoma to Seattle shortly after the Northern Pacific was completed September 8, 1883, but its terminal remained at Tacoma.

Hardly had the Puget Sound Shore R. R. become operable than Villard was forced to resign all three railroad presidencies due to financial difficulties in which he lost most of his personal fortune. Robert Harris took over the Northern Pacific, while Elijah Smith became President of the Oregon Railway & Navigation Co. and its two holding companies, and thus through them was President of the Columbia & Puget Sound and the Puget Sound Shore R. R. Now Harris of the Northern Pacific was a friend of C. B. Wright, head of the Tacoma Land Co., advocate of Tacoma as the principal

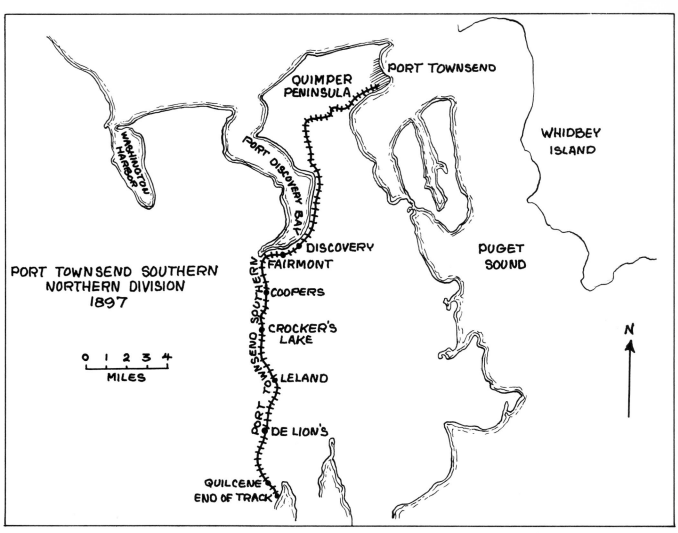

PORT TOWNSEND SOUTHERN
NORTHERN DIVISION
1897

0 1 2 3 4
MILES

WASHINGTON HARBOR

QUIMPER PENINSULA

PORT TOWNSEND

WHIDBEY ISLAND

PORT DISCOVERY BAY

PUGET SOUND

DISCOVERY
FAIRMONT
COOPERS
CROCKER'S LAKE
LELAND
DE LION'S

PORT TOWNSEND SOUTHERN

QUILCENE
END OF TRACK

N

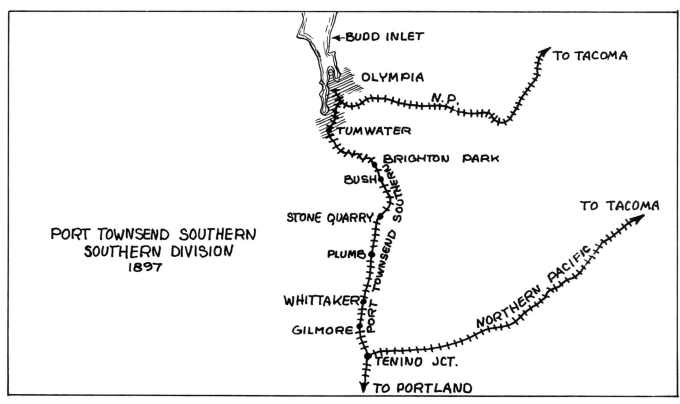

PORT TOWNSEND SOUTHERN
SOUTHERN DIVISION
1897

BUDD INLET

TO TACOMA

OLYMPIA

N.P.

TUMWATER

BRIGHTON PARK

BUSH

STONE QUARRY

PORT TOWNSEND SOUTHERN

TO TACOMA

PLUMB

WHITTAKER

GILMORE

NORTHERN PACIFIC

TENINO JCT.

TO PORTLAND

seaport and railroad center of Puget Sound, and of the building of a railroad over the Cascade Mountains to the Puyallup Valley and Tacoma from a point near Wallula, eliminating the long journey over the Oregon Railway & Navigation via Portland.

Harris soon ordered construction of the Cascade line, which was completed June, 1887, but in 1884, his first year at the helm of the Northern Pacific, he ordered train service between Tacoma and Stuck Jct. discontinued, leaving Seattle high and dry. Passengers arriving at Tacoma from the east had to lay overnight there and take the steamers to Seattle, for since the Puget Sound Shore R. R. had no rolling stock of its own, it could not operate. This so enraged the citizens of Seattle that they threatened condemnation proceedings, resulting in a half-hearted assent on the part of the Northern Pacific to operate the Puget Sound Shore trains into Tacoma from Stuck Jct. if they did not have to furnish the rolling stock. By rentals and later by purchase, the Puget Sound Shore acquired the locomotives and cars needed, and in 1885 service was resumed. Elijah Smith provided two trains daily between Tacoma and Seattle, and obviously business must have become very brisk, for in 1889 the Northern Pacific withdrew all opposition and purchased the Puget Sound Shore R. R. from Oregon & Transcontinental, combining it with their seven mile stretch between Stuck Jct. and Meeker, naming the combined lines the Northern Pacific & Puget Sound Shore R. R. The train service was increased to five daily in each direction, and Seattle was finally appeased.

In the meantime, Smith had extended the Columbia & Puget Sound to a new coal development at Franklin, 33 miles from Seattle in 1885, with branches to Lawson and Kummer, to insure a plentiful supply of coal for the Pacific Coast S. S. Co.'s colliers. Later, in 1892, another coal branch from Maple Valley to Taylor was added to the other coal feeders, and was the last new construction on the narrow gauge. Disaster struck the Columbia & Puget Sound on June 7, 1889, when the great Seattle fire, which destroyed a large portion of the city, burned the station, the shops and roundhouse, the coal bunkers and wharves, in fact, almost everything at the Columbia & Puget Sound Seattle terminal. Besides losing four freight cars, Locomotive No. 3, the GEO. C. BODE was destroyed, and a number of months passed before a new terminal and wharves could be constructed.

In 1890, with the Columbia & Puget Sound well launched on its career, Oregon Improvement Co., which by this time should have been dubbed the "Washington Improvement Co." (since most if its efforts at expansion were in Washington), became interested in the Port Townsend Southern R. R., which had been chartered September 28, 1887. Planned as a railroad on the west side of Puget Sound, from Port Townsend south to Olympia and eventually to Portland, this standard gauge railroad looked good to Oregon Improvement as a feeder for their lumber trade, and with funds provided in 1890 the line was completed south from Port Townsend for 27 miles to Quilcene, and there the work ceased. The orphan line was soon put to work hauling lumber to the steamers at Port Townsend, and it was never extended farther south.

As a part of this project, the 3 ft. gauge Olympia & Chehalis Valley R. R. was purchased by Oregon Improvement, the line to be standard gauged before acceptance. This change in gauge was made immediately, and became the Olympia Division of the Port Townsend Southern on September 11, 1890. This division had been built under the title of the Thurston County R. R. Constr. Co., incorporated June 4, 1877, and was completed from Olympia to Tenino and a junction with the Northern Pacific in July 1878, for a distance of 15 miles. Renamed the Olympia & Chehalis Valley R. R. on August 1, 1881, it operated under that name until taken over by the Port Townsend Southern. New standard gauge equipment was purchased for both divisions, though they lost money steadily from the official opening dates in 1890, and the idea of connecting the two divisions by additional construction was soon abandoned.

This was but one of the two losers sponsored by Oregon Improvement Co. in 1890, for they backed the Seattle & Northern R. R., which was completed from Anacortes, a port seventy miles north of Seattle on the east side of Puget Sound, to Hamilton, Washington, a distance of 35 miles on February 1, 1891. This road was also standard gauge, and produced more red ink on Oregon Improvement's

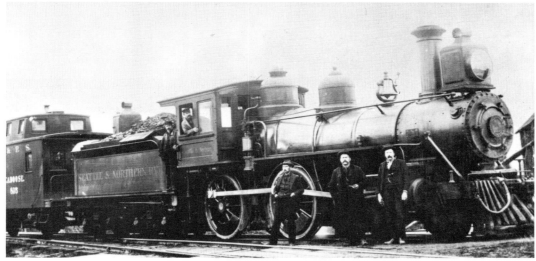

Columbia & Puget Sound lined up all its locomotives for a photo (opposite, top) near Renton, July 4, 1889. The HYAK, after service on the Walla Walla & Columbia River, is shown (opposite, middle) on the Seattle wharf, 1889. The BODE (opposite, bottom) was one of two saddle tankers built by Baldwin for the portage railroad. Port Townsend Southern Engine No. 6 (top) with unusual dual headlights, steams in Port Townsend station on a cold winter day, 1897, Seattle & Northern Engine No. 2, with a Columbia & Puget Sound caboose, is shown (above) at Anacortes, before 1899. A few years later, newly numbered for Great Northern, the same engine suffered a boiler explosion (below) at Mulkiteo, Washington. — Opposite, top: U. S. Forest Service; middle: Thomas Norrell; bottom: Herbert Broadbelt Collection; above: C. A. Mendenhall Collection; others, this page: D. H. Roberts Collection

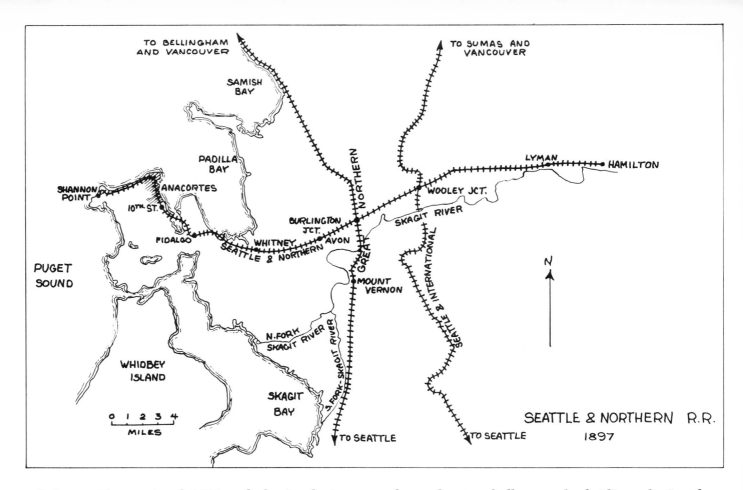

Seattle & Northern R.R. 1897

ledgers. The panic of 1893 and the hard times which followed brought Oregon Improvement Co. into receivership in 1895 after the October 1st coupons on their bond issue were defaulted. Reorganized in 1897 as the Pacific Coast Company, as previously related, the new management, headed by Hamilton W. Durand of New York, and with offices in Jersey City, New Jersey, set out to eliminate the loss producers and place the other units on a paying basis.

The first step was to standard gauge the Columbia & Puget Sound R. R., a step which was long overdue. This work was completed in November 1897, and by transferring unused locomotives and rolling stock from the Port Townsend Southern, and by purchasing new equipment, the Columbia & Puget Sound R. R. was in a position to exchange carload freight without transfer for the first time.

The Seattle & Northern, a continuous loser from the start, was next attended to. According to the annual report for 1901, the road was sold to the Great Northern for $450,000 cash, being 90% of its book value, yet actually only a small part of its original cost. The Great Northern in 1902 resold

the road to its wholly owned subsidiary, the Seattle & Montana R. R. for the net sum of $1,500,000. The Pacific Coast Co. seems to have been too much in a hurry to unload, in this case. They also unloaded large land holdings in Oregon and Washington, a city block in San Francisco, and various other real estate in an effort to raise cash and reduce taxes. The Alaska Ry. & Transp. Co., known as the Chilkoot Tramway, a cable tram used in connection with mining activities, was also sold at this time.

The Port Townsend Southern, after losing steadily during the first five years of the new management, was leased to the Northern Pacific in November, 1902, and was sold outright to them for $375,000 on July 1, 1914, although this sum applied only to the Olympia Division, the Port Townsend Division being leased separately by the Northern Pacific to C. J. Ericksen of Seattle for 15 years, under the name of Port Townsend & Puget Sound Ry. Ericksen soon abandoned the section from Quilcene to Discovery Junction, the latter being the terminal of the Seattle, Port Angeles & Western Ry. a newly built subsidiary of the Milwaukee. In

1945, R. S. Fox, of Seattle, bought this ten mile remainder, and operates it today as the Port Townsend R. R.

The year 1902 also marked the end of a long dispute over trackage ownership of the Columbia & Puget Sound Ry. between Black River Junction and Argo. The Northern Pacific claimed this track belonged to them, but an amicable settlement was reached whereby both roads divided the right-of-way in half, right down the center of the track. A new standard gauge track for the Columbia & Puget Sound was laid to the east of the existing track, and paid for by the Northern Pacific, which then moved the old track west of the dividing line. Another agreement signed in 1903 exchanged tracks and terminals between Argo and Seattle. The Northern Pacific got the Columbia & Puget Sound tracks from Argo to King Street station, while the latter received the old Puget Sound Shore tracks from Argo to Atlantic Street, affording a direct connection with the Pacific Coast S. S. Co.'s waterfront properties. A new roundhouse and shops for the Columbia & Puget Sound were built the same year, on the land end of the great coal dock on the waterfront. This was an unusual railroad terminal, with the back of the roundhouse facing the street, and the turntable and roundhouse leads on the pier facing towards the Sound.

In 1906, the Milwaukee Ry., building its Pacific Coast Extension from the Dakotas to Seattle, entered into a joint agreement with the Columbia & Puget Sound to use its tracks from Maple Valley to Seattle, a distance of 23 miles. Signing a 99 year lease, the Columbia & Puget Sound agreed to double-track the line and equip it with electric block signals. In December 1909, a joint track agreement with the Oregon & Washington R. R., a subsidiary of the Union Pacific was signed, and the section from Black River Junction to Seattle became the main line of three railroads. Not for long, however, for the Union Pacific shortly afterwards built its own line and left the Milwaukee as the sole lessor of the Columbia & Puget Sound.

In 1910, the Columbia & Puget Sound placed an order on American Locomotive Co. for three new engines, a 4-4-0 for passenger service, a 2-8-0 for the freights, and an 0-6-0 for yard service. These were the last locomotives to be purchased by the Company, the last two working to the end of steam in 1953. In 1916, the year of the sale of the steamships to H. F. Alexander, the name of the railroad was changed to Pacific Coast Railroad. With a "Railway" in California and a "Railroad" in Washington, there was bound to be confusion, but it mattered little because their gauges were not the same. This was the year the Cashier of the Pacific Coast Co. absconded with most of the surplus cash, the loss after insurance amounting to $100,000. In spite of this setback, the company showed a profit through most of its years. The dividends were erratic, but when they paid a dividend, it usually was a whopper. None were paid between 1916 and 1924, but in that year a 58¾% melon was cut. In 1935 a 120% dividend established an all-time record, and while none were paid in World War II years, 25% was disbursed in 1947, 48% in 1948, and 33.8% in 1951.

Several of the coal mine spurs were abandoned prior to 1933, but in that year, with the coal business suffering from competition with crude oil and natural gas, and some of the mines having been worked out, the Newcastle branch was abandoned, followed by most of the Taylor branch in 1945, leaving only the Maple Valley-Seattle section over which the traffic of the Milwaukee dwarfed the freight-only business of the Pacific Coast R. R. The latter thus settled down to being an industrial switching railroad in effect, and a prosperous one to this day, fulfilling its destiny and justifying the efforts of Seattle's pioneers.

It should be a pleasure for the reader to hear of at least one segment of the vast empire of Oregon Improvement Co. which still has a future, for the Pacific Coast R. R. fared so well that in 1951 the Great Northern invested a considerable sum to acquire stock control of what had been just a short-line, when Great Northern reached Seattle. Shortly after, the last steam locomotive was retired, and at this writing, a plan for the merger of Great Northern, Northern Pacific and Pacific Coast is before the Interstate Commerce Commission. If this consolidation is approved, the one surviving caboose and seventy freight cars still carried in the equipment register of the Pacific Coast R. R. will be swallowed up for all time.

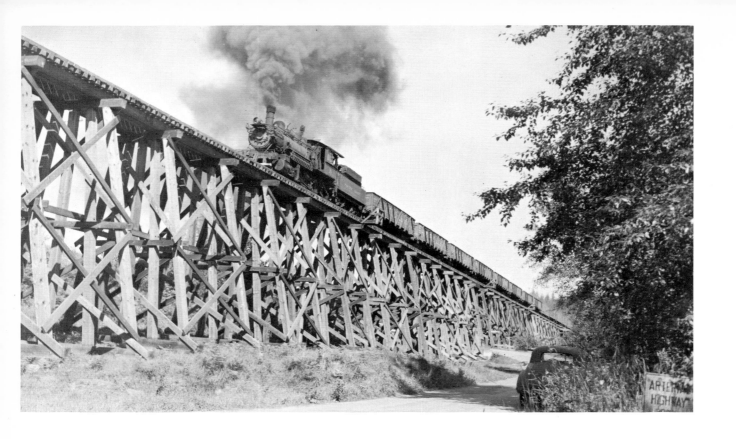

Engine No. 16 crosses Bridge 22.8, near Maple Valley on the Black Diamond branch (*above*). No. 15 passes under the covered bridge near Black River, which has since burned and been removed. Both pictures were taken in 1951, just before Diesels replaced the last steam engines. —*Albert Farrow*

Engine No. 15 is by the old station in Renton *(above),* now replaced by a smaller building. No. 16 spews black smoke from soft coal near Maple Valley. These were also in the last days of steam. — *Albert Farrow*

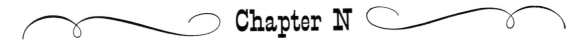

Chapter N

The Locomotives and Rolling Stock of the Washington Railroads

THE LOCOMOTIVE ROSTERS which follow include the narrow gauge Columbia & Puget Sound, the Olympia & Chehalis Valley, and the three standard gauge lines. The roster of the Columbia & Puget Sound contained a polyglot mixture of types and builders. When the Seattle & Walla Walla was completed, there were three locomotives on the line, No. 1 being a Wm. Mason bogie type of 0-6-4 wheel arrangement, built for a "never built" railroad, the Stockton & Ione, in California. No. 2 was a tiny 4-4-0 built by W. H. Bailey & Co., known also as the National Locomotive Works, at Connellsville, Pennsylvania in 1877. The third locomotive was Seattle Coal's ANT, rented from that road during tracklaying operations and retained after the line was opened. The other two locomotives of the Seattle Coal & Transp. Co. were taken over in 1878, making five locomotives on the Seattle & Walla Walla at that time. Not listed in the Columbia & Puget Sound roster is an 0-4-0 saddle tanker ordered by Seattle Coal from Baldwin and delivered in July 1877. This engine, named the SEATTLE, was Baldwin No. 4108, and was built for 30 inch gauge, so it is presumed to have been used at the Newcastle mines, for there is no further record of it.

After the Columbia & Puget Sound was organized in 1880, two locomotives were purchased from the Walla Walla & Columbia River R. R., arriving in July 1881 to become Columbia & Puget Sound Nos. 6 and 7. The Union Pacific records state they were purchased by J. W. Sprague for Northern Pacific R. R. construction projects and for the Columbia & Puget Sound. Sprague was a contractor who worked for Villard, and his work involved all of the railroads of which Villard was President, and anything Sprague purchased might turn up on any of these railroads. In May 1883, the ANT, too light for the work then required of it, was sold to a lumber company, and in December 1883, Pacific Coast Railway No. 1, the AVILA, equipped with a tender, converted to an 0-6-0 switcher and with saddle tank removed, arrived aboard the steamer *Walla Walla* to become Columbia & Puget Sound's 2nd No. 5. There is one mystery of 1883 which has never been solved. On August 31, 1883, the Seattle *Post-Intelligencer* noted that "A narrow gauge locomotive and tender from the West Side Division of the Oregon Railway & Navigation Co. is awaiting shipment from Ainsworth Dock in Portland for the Columbia & Puget Sound R. R." The same paper on September 11 noted that "A new narrow gauge locomotive is here from the Oregon Railway. It arrived on September 8th."

The West Side Division was a part of Villard's Oregon & California R. R., not the Oregon Railway & Navigation, and the only narrow gauge section was the Oregonian Ry. This road had eight locomotives at the time, and this mystery engine could have been any one of these. The fact that the Columbia & Puget Sound bought a new consolidation from Baldwin in 1885 and numbered it No. 8 would indicate that this mystery engine lasted only a short time, if it was used at all. The annual report for Oregon Improvement Co. for 1886 lists eight locomotives on the Columbia & Puget Sound, and all are accounted for.

When the Olympia & Chehalis Valley was standard gauged in 1890, the narrow gauge equipment was surplus, and was shipped to the Columbia & Puget Sound in May, 1891. Engine No. 1 became Columbia & Puget Sound No. 10, but there is no evidence that Olympia & Chehalis Valley No. 3 ever ran on the Columbia & Puget Sound at any time. In 1889, the GEO. C. BODE No. 3 was lost in the Seattle fire, and was replaced by a second-hand Brooks mogul from the Union Pacific. No. 4 was replaced by another from the same source a few months later.

The decision to standard gauge the Columbia & Puget Sound was made in 1896, and at that time No. 5 was sold, the purchaser having the option to buy No. 6 in 1898 after standard gauging was completed. Except for 4-4-0 No. 2 and HYAK No. 7, which were listed as stored, not sold, in the 1898 annual report, the other narrow gauge engines and most of the rolling stock were sold to the contractor then building the White Pass & Yukon R. R. in Alaska. Two of these engines are still in existence, on display at Dawson in Yukon Territory, and Whitehorse.

Seattle & Walla Walla Engine No. 1 is at Seattle wharf. — *D. H. Roberts Collection*

Columbia & Puget Sound Engine No. 5 was converted from saddle tanker to switch engine. It was originally the AVILA, first locomotive on San Luis Obispo & Santa Maria Valley. — *Williamson's Marine Photo Shop*

COLUMBIA & PUGET SOUND (3 ft. gauge)

Locomotives

No.	Type	Builder	Constr. No.	Date Blt.	Drivers	Cyls.	Total Weight
1	0-6-4	Wm. Mason	552	8/1875	33	13x16	50000
2	4-4-0	W. H. Bailey	—	5/1877	36	9x16	26000
3	2-6-2T	Baldwin	3603	5/1874	30	9x12	20000
2nd 3	2-6-0	Brooks	—	1881	42	14½x18	57400
4	0-6-0T	Baldwin	3713	4/1875	30	9x12	20000
2nd 4	2-6-0	Brooks	—	1881	42	14½x18	57400
5	0-4-0T	Fulton Fdry. S.F.	—	9/1871	—	6x12	14000
2nd 5	0-6-0	Baldwin	3771	8/1875	36	10x16	36000(approx.)
6	2-6-0	Porter-Bell	292	2/1878	36	11x16	36000
7	0-4-0T	Porter-Bell	114	2/1872	—	8x16	15000
8	2-8-0	Baldwin	7597	5/1885	37½	15x20	63000
9	2-8-0	Grant	—	8/1882	36	15½x20	63000
10	4-4-0	Baldwin	4294	3/1878	42	12x16	43300

Notes:

No. 1 Named A. A. DENNY. Built for Stockton & Ione No. 2, AMADOR. Returned to factory and resold to Seattle & Walla Walla No. 1, 10/1876. To Columbia & Puget Sound No. 1, 11/1880. Retired 1895 and boiler used in stationary service, Seattle shops.

No. 2 Named AL-KI. Built as Seattle & Walla Walla No. 2. To Columbia & Puget Sound No. 2, 11/1880. Retired 1897.

No. 3 Named GEO. C. BODE. Built as 0-6-0T for Seattle Coal & Transp. Co. No. 2. To Seattle & Walla Walla No. 3, 2/1878 and rebuilt to a 2-6-2T. To Columbia & Puget Sound No. 3, 11/1880. Destroyed in Seattle fire of June 7, 1889.

2nd No. 3 Ex Union Pacific, earlier Utah & Northern. Acq. 11/1889. Sold to White Pass & Yukon No. 1 - 1897. Now on display at Whitehorse, Y. T., as W. P. & Y. No. 51.

No. 4 Named GEORGINA. Built as Seattle Coal & Transp. Co. No. 3. To Seattle & Walla Walla No. 4, 2/1878. To Columbia & Puget Sound No. 4, 11/1880. Gone by 1890.

2nd No. 4 Ex Union Pacific-Utah & Northern. Acq. 1890. Sold to White Pass & Yukon No. 2 - 1897. Later No. 52. Scrapped 1923.

No. 5 Named ANT. Built as Seattle Coal Co. No. 1. To Seattle Coal & Transp. Co. No. 1; to Seattle & Walla Walla in 1877. Became No. 5 in 1878. To Columbia & Puget Sound No. 5, 11/1880; to Ordway & Weidler, 5/1883; to Mosquito & Coal Creek R.R., 10/1883; to Long-Bell Corp., 1923. Scrapped in the 1940s.

2nd No. 5 From Pacific Coast Ry. No. 1, 12/1883. Converted from 2-4-2T to 0-6-0 tender engine. Sold 7/29/1896 to Mike Earles for Puget Sound Sawmill & Shingle Co., Port Crescent, Wash. Later Puget Sound Mill & Tbr. Co.

No. 6 From Walla Walla & Columbia River No. 6, J. W. LADD, 7/1881. Renamed RAINIER. Presumed sold to Mike Earles in 1898.

No. 7 From Walla Walla & Columbia River No. 1, WALLA WALLA, 7/1881. Renamed HYAK. On the road until the end of narrow gauge, 12/1897.

No. 8 Bought new. Sold to White Pass & Yukon No. 5 - 1897. Later became Klondike Mines No. 2, Dawson, Y. T. Now on display there.

No. 9 Acq. 2nd-hand in 1887 from Grant. Built as Toledo, Cincinnati & St. Louis No. 63. Sold to White Pass & Yukon No. 3 - 1897. Scrapped as No. 53 in 1918.

No. 10 From Olympia & Chehalis Valley No. 1, E. H. QUIMETTE. Acq. 5/1891. Sold to White Pass & Yukon No. 4 - 1897. Sold to Tanana Valley No. 50 - 1907. Later Alaska R.R. No. 50. Scrapped 1930.

C. & P.S. Engine No. 9 (top) was a Grant consolidation, photographed at Seattle in the 1890s. No. 10 (above) had formerly been on the Olympia & Chehalis Valley, also pho-tographed at Seattle. Engine No. 12 hauls a train out of Seattle (below), 1908. — Above, both: Williamson's Marine Photo Shop; below: Fred Jukes

OLYMPIA & CHEHALIS VALLEY (3 ft. gauge)

Locomotives

No.	Type	Builder	Constr. No.	Date Blt.	Drivers	Cyls.	Total Weight
1	4-4-0	Baldwin	4294	3/1878	42	12x16	43300
2	Unknown						
2	0-4-0T	Porter-Bell	124	2/1872	—	8x16	15000
3	2-6-0	Baldwin	7298	5/1884	37	12x16	38000

Notes:

No. 1 Left Baldwin lettered "Olympia & Tenino," name E. H. QUIMETTE. To Columbia & Puget Sound No. 10, 5/1891.

No. 2 Nothing is known of this engine except 1879 and 1880 reports list two locomotives on the line. Apparently sold by 12/1881.

2nd No. 2 From Walla Walla & Columbia River No. 2, WALLULA. Acq. 12/1881. Destroyed by fire at Tenino roundhouse 6/10/1889.

No. 3 Bought new. Named OLYMPIA. Delivered to Columbia & Puget Sound 5/1891. Further history unknown.

PORT TOWNSEND SOUTHERN (Standard gauge)

Locomotives

No.	Type	Builder	Constr. No.	Date Blt.	Drivers	Cyls.	Total Weight
1	4-4-0	New York	628	7/1890	62	17x24	78000
2	4-4-0	New York	629	7/1890	62	17x24	78000
3	4-6-0	Baldwin	11280	10/1890	54	17x24	80000
4	4-6-0	Baldwin	11265	10/1890	54	17x24	80000
5	4-4-0	See note					
6	2-4-2T	Porter	1784	10/1897	40	10x16	41000

Notes:

No. 1 on Olympia Division until 1897. To Columbia & Puget Sound No. 5 - 1897. To Seattle & Northern, 1898-1901. To Columbia & Puget Sound No. 5, 1901. Probably not on Port Townsend Southern as No. 5.

No. 2 ran on both Olympia and Port Townsend Divisions. To Columbia & Puget Sound No. 9 in 1897.

No. 3 On Port Townsend Division. Became Northern Pacific No. 369 in 1902.

No. 4 On Port Townsend Division until 1897. To Columbia & Puget Sound No. 4, 1897.

No. 5 Doubtful if this engine ever ran on the Port Townsend Southern as No. 5.

No. 6 On Olympia Division. Went with the road to the N.P. in 1902. Later sold to Rogue River Valley No. 6. Became Portland & Oregon City No. 6 in 1915.

SEATTLE & NORTHERN (Standard gauge)

Locomotives

No.	Type	Builder	Constr. No.	Date Built	Drivers	Cyls.	Total Weight
1	4-4-0	R. Norris	—	1866	62	17x22	70000
2	4-4-0	New York	627	7/1890	62	17x24	78000

Notes:

No. 1 Original owner unknown. Acq. 1890 during construction of the road. To Columbia & Puget Sound No. 1, 1897 in exchange for Port Townsend Southern No. 1.

No. 2 To Seattle & Montana Ry. in 1902. To Great Northern 2nd 139. Blew up at Mulkiteo, Washington.

PUGET SOUND SHORE (Standard gauge)

Locomotives

No.	Type	Builder	Constr. No.	Date Built	Drivers	Cyls.	Total Weight
1	4-4-0	Pittsburgh	862	4/1888	62	17x24	—
366	4-4-0	Baldwin	10692	3/1890	—	—	—

Notes:

No. 1 was renumbered Northern Pacific 367 in 1890 and was later Northern Pacific 804.

No. 366 was ordered by the Puget Sound Shore R.R. but received a Northern Pacific road number. It was later Northern Pacific 740.

COLUMBIA & PUGET SOUND (Standard gauge)
Later PACIFIC COAST RAILROAD

Locomotives

No.	Type	Builder	Constr. No.	Date Built	Drivers	Cyls.	Total Weight
1	4-4-0	R. Norris	—	1866	62	17x22	70000
4	4-6-0	Baldwin	11265	10/1890	54	17x24	80000
5	4-4-0	New York	628	7/1890	62	17x24	78000
7	2-8-0	Baldwin	15439	7/1897	50	19x24	115000
8	2-8-0	Baldwin	15440	7/1897	50	19x24	115000
9	4-4-0	New York	629	7/1890	62	17x24	78000
10	0-6-0	Baldwin	15501	9/1897	50	17x24	80000
11	2-8-0	Baldwin	19298	7/1901	50	19x24	121650
12	2-8-0	Baldwin	22759	8/1903	50	19x24	121650
14	2-8-0	Alco-Rh. Is.	41965	2/1907	52	20x24	124500
15	2-8-0	Alco-Rh. Is.	41966	2/1907	52	20x24	124500
16	2-8-0	Alco-Brooks	48294	7/1910	52	20x24	128000
17	0-6-0	Alco-Brooks	48296	7/1910	51	19x26	127000
18	4-4-0	Alco-Brooks	48295	7/1910	62	18x24	110000

Notes:

There were no locomotives numbered 2, 3, 6 or 13 at any time.

No. 1 Ex Seattle & Northern No. 1. Acq. 1897. Sold in 1900 to W. D. Hofius, Seattle.

No. 4 Ex Port Townsend Southern No. 4. Acq. 1897. Sold to M. J. Henney for the Copper River & Northwestern R.R. 1906.

No. 5 Ex Port Townsend Southern No. 5. Acq. 1897. Traded to Seattle & Northern for their No. 1. Returned as Columbia & Puget Sound No. 5 in 1902. Sold to Neider J. Marcus in 1923. Scrapped 3/43.

No. 7 Sold to McKenna Lbr. Co. No. 7, 5/1916 for $6,000.

No. 8 Sold to Northwestern Steel Co. for scrap - 1938.

No. 9 Ex Port Townsend Southern No. 2. Acq. 1897. Wrecked at Argo - 1908. Scrapped 1910.

No. 10 Sold to Port of Seattle No. 10 - 1941. To U.S.A. No. 4032 1/1942.

No. 11 Sold to Northwestern Steel Co. for scrap - 1938.

No. 12 Sold to Dulien Steel Products Co. for scrap - 1950.

No. 14 Sold for scrap - 1951.

No. 15 Sold for scrap - 1953.

No. 16 Sold for scrap - 1953.

No. 17 Sold for scrap - 1951.

No. 18 Sold to Japan for scrap - 1939.

STANDARD GAUGE PASSENGER CARS OWNED BY THE
COLUMBIA & PUGET SOUND RAILROAD

No.	Type	Date Built	Builder	No. Seats	Remarks
A-1	Business	1891	Pullman	8	Acq. from N.P. 1901. To Alaska R.R. - 1922
1	Combination	1890	Billmeyer & Small	—	Assigned to Seattle & Northern To Seattle & Montana R.R.
2	Coach	1890	"	—	Assigned to Seattle & Northern To Seattle & Montana R.R.
3	Baggage-Mail	1890	"	—	Ex PTS No. 3. Changed to milk car. Sold 1919 to City of Prineville Ry.
4	Coach	1890	"	52	Ex PTS No. 4. Sold to Wood & Iverson 12/1916
5	Coach	1890	"	52	Ex PTS No. 5. Sold to Wood & Iverson 12/1916
6	Combination	1890	"	—	Remained on PTS. Went to Northern Pacific in 1902.
7	Coach	1890	"	52	Ex PTS No. 7. Changed to combo—30 seats, 6/17. To Wood & Iverson, 5/1923
8	Baggage-Mail	1905	C. & P. S. Shops	—	Sold to W. E. Mahaffey, 7/1923.
9	Combination	1909	Harlan & Hollingsworth	40	Scrapped 1935
10	Coach	1909	"	64	Scrapped 1935
11	Coach	1909	"	64	Changed to combo—48 seats, 10/1914. Originally half smoker, half ladies only
12	Coach	1909	"	58	Gone by 1946

Notes:

Cars Nos. 1 and 2 were assigned to the Seattle & Northern. Nos. 3 to 7 inclusive were assigned to the Port Townsend Southern. In 1897, cars 3 to 5 and 7 were relettered Columbia & Puget Sound, as were cars 8 to 12 inclusive, as built. All were relettered Pacific Coast Railroad in 1916, unless previously sold.

PACIFIC COAST RAILROAD
Freight equipment, including the 1916 renumbering.

Class	C. & P.S. Nos.	P.C. RR Nos.	Remarks
Caboose	820, 812-817	50-56	Orig. 3 ft. ga. 818 retired 1907. 819 retired 1910
Gravel-Side Dump	700-711 (706-11 from old flats)	101-111	Renumb. 740-751 prior 1929.
Box	131, 139-149	131, 139-149	See Note A
Flat, Work	300-318 (300-313 ex 3 ft. ga.)	314, 318	No. 318 later renumbered No. 813. Others scrapped by 1913.
Coal, Hopper	400-600, 601-635	400-635	—
Bottom	—	636	No. 636 purchased from Seattle & Rainier Valley
Gondola	1260-1279, 1285	800-812	Only 46 cars left in this series in 1916.

PACIFIC COAST RAILROAD FREIGHT EQUIPMENT — *Continued*

Class	C. & P.S. Nos.	P.C. RR Nos.	Remarks
Caboose	1286, 1287	820, 821	No. 1285 later became No. 850.
	1202-1257	—	—
	1296-1366	830-875	—
	—	915-942	Purchased from Skinner & Eddy Ship-yards.
Wood Racks	202-299	1400-1417	Renumb. 1450-67 by 1929.
Flat	320-365	1500-1540	—
Gondola	900-914	2000-2014	Renumb. 2050-2065 by 1929.
Gondola-Drop Btm.	750-765	3000-3014	—
Box	120-129, 191-200	4000-4019	Renumb. 4080-4099 by 1929. All blt. from old flat cars.
Box	150-190	4540-4540	See Note A
Air Dump	1001-1010	1001-1010	—
Derrick	1000	1000, 215	No. 215 added after 1916.
Pile Driver	—	259	—

Note A:

Boxcars rebuilt as follows: No. 130 to 186; No. 132 to No. 190; No. 134 to No. 187; No. 135 scrapped; No. 136 to No. 188; No. 137 to No. 189. The shops rebuilt gondolas, flats, wood racks, boxcars and built new cars, some of them going to the Pacific Coast Ry. in California.

SEATTLE & NORTHERN
Freight Cars

Box	Total — 4	Nos. 2-5	To Great Northern R.R. 1902
Flats	Total — 10	?	To Great Northern R.R. 1902
Logging	Total — 16	?	To Great Northern R.R. 1902
Trucks	—	—	—

— *C. T. Steeb*

Columbia & Puget Sound Engine No. 18 *(opposite, top)*, later Pacific Coast Railroad No. 18, was photographed at Black Diamond before 1916. Pacific Coast No. 16 *(opposite, middle)*, was the only one of its class, Maple Valley, 1939. No. 17 *(opposite, bottom)*, survived, switching at Seattle, to the very end of steam operation. P.C.R.R. No. 10 *(above)*, Seattle, 1940. No. 14 *(below)* was one of two Rhode Island built Alcos, Seattle, 1949. — *Opposite, top: D. H. Roberts Collection; all others: Albert Farrow*

Pacific Coast Railroad Engine No. 18 was photographed at Seattle, 1924.

Gondolas, like this one, traveled between Seattle and the coal mining region. There was no doubt as to the ownership of these boxcars *(bottom) at Seattle. — Both: C. T. Steeb*

INDEX

PACIFIC COAST RAILWAY COMPANY
TIME TABLE NO. 37
MAY 4, 1913

West-bound trains are superior to trains of the same class in the opposite direction. See Rule 81.

EAST BOUND — FROM PORT SAN LUIS								WEST BOUND — TO PORT SAN LUIS			
Second Class		**First Class**						**First Class**		**Second Class**	
8 Freight	6 Mixed	4 Mail & Express	2 Passenger	Miles from Port San Luis	STATIONS	Miles from Los Olivos	Siding Cap. (cars)	1 Passenger	3 Mail & Express	5 Mixed	7 Freight
Leave Daily	Leave Daily	Leave Daily	Leave Daily					Arrive Daily	Arrive Daily	Arrive Daily	Arrive Daily
	12.30 PM				D PORT SAN LUIS W T	76.1	146			11.55 AM	6.05 PM
					0.3						
	12.32			0.3	f HOTEL MARRE	75.8				11.53	
					1.7						
	12.37			2.0	f AVILA	74.0	47			11.46	
					1.4						
	12.46			3.4	f SPRINGS	72.7				11.39	
					0.6						
	12.50			4.0	f MILES	72.1	19			11.35	
					6.3						
9.10 AM	1.10 PM	2.45 PM	6.30 AM	10.3	D SAN LUIS OBISPO W C T	65.8	110	10.45 AM	2.20 PM	11.15 AM	
					1.1						
9.13		2.50	6.33	11.4	f S. P. JUNCTION	64.7	18	10.41	2.13		
					0.7						
		3.05	6.45	12.1	S. P. DEPOT	65.4	12	10.38	2.10		
					0.7						
		3.08	6.48	11.4	f S. P. JUNCTION	64.7	18	10.33	2.01		
					4.5						
9.30		3.20	6.59	15.9	f STEELE'S	60.2	23	10.21	1.48		5.45
					1.5						
9.35		3.24	7.03	17.4	f BITUMINA	58.7	60	10.17	1.44		5.40
					0.5						
9.45					f HADLEY		22				5.35
					4.9						
10.03		3.38	7.17	22.3	f VERDE	54.1	15	10.03	1.30		5.15
					3.2						
10.35		3.49	7.27	25.5	D ARROYO GRANDE	50.6	91	9.53	1.19		5.00
					4.6						
10.55		4.02	7.40	30.1	f BERROS	46.0	17	9.40	1.05		4.38
					1.8						
11.05		4.10	7.46	31.9	f SUMMIT	44.2	12	9.33	12.58		4.28
					2.8						
11.15		4.18	7.54	34.7	D NIPOMO W	41.4	30	9.26	12.50		4.18
					7.0						
11.55		4.40	8.20	41.7	D SANTA MARIA W	34.4	94	9.06	12.30		3.50
					1.7						
12.01 PM		4.42	8.25	43.4	D SUEY JUNCTION y	32.7		9.00	12.17		2.50 PM
					0.3						
		4.46		43.7	f UNION	32.4			12.15		
					2.0						
		4.53	8.33	45.7	f LAKE VIEW	30.4	16	8.54	12.10		
					2.3						
		5.04	8.38 AM	48.0	D ORCUTT	28.1	40	8.48 AM	12.05		
					0.5						
		5.06		48.5	f GRACIOSA c	27.6	10		11.59		
					2.1						
		5.14		50.6	f DIVIDE	25.5	14		11.44		
					2.0						
		5.23		52.6	f BICKNELL	23.5	10		11.34		
					2.4						
		5.33		55.0	f HARRIS	21.1	19		11.24		
					3.4						
		5.45		58.4	f CARREAGA	17.7	8		11.10		
					2.0						
				60.4	f ORENA	15.7	8				
					3.4						
		6.07		63.8	D LOS ALAMOS W	12.3	24		10.52		
					4.0						
		6.19		67.8	f WIGMORE	8.3	15		10.37		
					5.0						
				72.8	f ZACA	3.3	19		10.22		
					3.3						
		6.50 PM		76.1	D LOS OLIVOS T		47		10.10 AM		
Leave Daily	Leave Daily	Arrive Daily	Arrive Daily					Leave Daily	Leave Daily	Leave Daily	Leave Daily

COLUMBIA & PUGET SOUND RAILROAD CO.

SUMMER TIME SCHEDULE

TAKING EFFECT SUNDAY, MAY 1ST, 1910

MAIN LINE

Northbound (to Seattle)

	No. 31 PASSENGER DAILY EXCEPT SUNDAY	No. 33 PASSENGER DAILY	Special (E) PASSENGER Sunday Only	Special (D) PASSENGER Sunday Only	*Special (A) PASSENGER SATURDAY AND SUNDAY ONLY
	A. M.	P. M.	A. M.		P. M.
SEATTLE Ar.	8.50	1.45	8.50	Ar 12.44 P.M	7.50
BLACK RIVER	8.20	1.20	8.20	12.32	7.25
EARLINGTON	8.13	1.15	8.13	12.25	7.20
RENTON	8.10	1.12	Lv. 8.10 A.M.	12.15	7.18
ELLIOTT	7.52	1.03			7.08
CEDAR MOUNTAIN	7.42	12.55			7.00
MAPLE VALLEY	7.31	Lv 12.45p M			Lv 5.20 Ar 5.20
HENRYS	7.17				*5.07
BLACK DIAMOND	7.10				*5.00
FRANKLIN Lv.	6.50				*4.51
	A. M.	P. M.		P. M.	P. M.

Special (E): From Newcastle Branch

Special (D): To Seattle as No. 33

No. 33: From Maple Valley Daily Except Sunday through from Franklin

*On Sundays Special A will be 1 hr. 20 min. late on above schedule Franklin to Maple Valley, going through from Maple Valley on time without layover.

Southbound (to Franklin)

	No. 36 MIXED DAILY EXCEPT SATURDAY AND SUNDAY	Special (B) PASSENGER Saturday Only	Special (C) PASSENGER Sunday Only	Special (F) PASSENGER Sunday Only	Special* (G) PASSENGER SATURDAY AND SUNDAY ONLY	No. 34 PASSENGER DAILY EXCEPT SATURDAY & SUNDAY	No. 32 PASSENGER Daily
	P. M.	P. M.	A.M.	P. M.	P. M.	P. M.	A. M.
SEATTLE Lv.	3.00	11.35		6.20	3.00	5.20	9.30
BLACK RIVER	3.32	12.00	Lv 10.31 A.M.	6.45	3.25	5.45	9.54
EARLINGTON	3.36	12.04	10.43	6.49	3.28	5.48	9.57
RENTON	Ar 3.45 P.M	12.08	10.50	Ar 6.52 P.M.	3.38	5.58	10.00
ELLIOTT		12.17	11.00		3.55	6.15	10.12
CEDAR MOUNTAIN		12.25			4.03	6.23	10.20
MAPLE VALLEY		12.35			*4.15	6.35	Ar 10.30 A.M.
HENRYS		12.48			*4.28	6.48	
BLACK DIAMOND		12.55			*4.38	6.58	
FRANKLIN Ar.		1.10			*4.50	7.10	
	P. M.	A. M.	A. M.		P. M.	P. M.	

No. 36: To Newcastle Branch — Saturdays Special G Connects

Special (C): From Seattle as No. 32

Special (F): To Newcastle Branch

No. 32: To Maple Valley Branch Daily Except Sundays — Sundays Through To Franklin

*On Sundays Special G runs via Taylor and will be 1 hr. 20 min. late Maple Valley to Franklin on above schedule.

MAPLE VALLEY BRANCH

	Special (306) PASSENGER SUNDAY ONLY	Special (206) PASSENGER SATURDAY ONLY	No. 32 PASSENGER DAILY EXCEPT SUNDAY	No. 33 PASSENGER DAILY EXCEPT SUNDAY	Special (203) PASSENGER SATURDAY ONLY	Special (205) PASSENGER SATURDAY ONLY	Special (307) PASSENGER SUNDAY ONLY
	P. M.	P. M.	A. M.	P. M.	A. M.	P. M.	P. M.
Lv. Seattle Ar.	(a) 3.00	(a) 3.00	9.30	1.45	(3l) 8.50	(A) 7.50	(A) 7.50
Ar. Maple Valley Lv.	(a) 4.15	(a) 4.15	10.30	12.45	(3l) 7.31	(A) 6.50	(A) 6.50
Lv. Maple Valley Ar.	4.16	5.21	10.31	12.44	7.28	6.39	5.34
Hobart	4.25	5.30	10.43	12.28	7.12	6.25	5.20
Walsh	4.34	5.39	10.53	12.18	7.02	6.15	5.10
Sherwood	4.44	5.49	11.02	12.09	6.53	6.06	5.01
Ar. Taylor Lv.	4.50	5.55	11.10	12.01	6.45	5.58	4.53
	P. M.	P. M.	A. M.	P. M.	A. M.	P. M.	P. M.

See Special A.   See Special G

NEWCASTLE BRANCH

	Special (F) PASSENGER SUNDAY ONLY	No. 36 MIXED DAILY EXCEPT SUNDAY	No. 35 MIXED DAILY
	P. M.	P. M.	A. M.
Lv. Seattle Ar.	(F) 6.20	3.00	(3l E) 8.50
Ar. Renton Lv.	(F) 6.52	3.45	(3l E) 8.10
Lv. Renton Ar.	6.55	3.55	8.05
Kennydale	7.04	4.10	7.52
Newcastle	7.14	4.25	7.40
Ar Coal Creek Lv.	7.20	4.40	7.30
	P. M.	P. M.	A. M.

C. D. DUNANN, Gen. Pass. Agt.

G. W. MERTENS, Supt.